Skillful Rowing

Edward McNeely/Marlene Royle

Skillful Rowing

Meyer & Meyer Sport

British Library Cataloguing in Publication Data
A catalogue record for this book is available from the British Library

McNeely/Royle:
Skillful Rowing/Edward McNeely; Marlene Royle
Oxford: Meyer & Meyer Sport (UK) Ltd., 2002
ISBN 1-84126-084-3

© 2002 by Meyer & Meyer Sport (UK) Ltd.
Aachen, Adelaide, Auckland, Budapest, Graz, Johannesburg,
Miami, Olten (CH), Oxford, Singapore, Toronto
Member of the World
Sports Publishers' Association (WSPA)
www.w-s-p-a.org

Printed and bound by Vimperk AG
ISBN 1-84126-084-3
E-Mail: verlag@meyer-meyer-sports.com
www.meyer-meyer-sports.com

Contents

9

Throughout this book, the pronouns he, she, him, her and so on are interchangeable and intended to be inclusive of both men and women. It is important in sport, as elsewhere, that men and women have equal status and opportunities.

Chapter 1:
Aerobic Training

Developing a high level of aerobic fitness is the key to rowing performance. To bring more accuracy to aerobic training programs sport scientists and coaches have developed a system of aerobic training categories. While there are as many versions of the training category system as there are countries using it, the physiological basis for the training systems are the same throughout the world.

1.1 Physiology of Training Categories

Most, if not all, of the category systems rely on the blood lactate response to exercise. Lactate, or lactic acid, is a substance produced by the muscles when the anaerobic energy systems become involved in an activity. Measuring lactate at various workloads determines where the anaerobic system becomes an important part of energy production. The two physiological markers that are found through a lactate test are aerobic threshold and anaerobic threshold. These, combined with VO_2 max are the backbone of training category systems.

1.1.1 VO₂ max

VO_2 max is the maximum amount of oxygen that the body can take in and use. There is a strong correlation between VO_2 max and 2000 m rowing ergometer performance. Exercise at VO_2 max can only be done for a short period of time before fatigue sets in. Most people won't be able to hold this intensity for more than 4-5 minutes. In order to be successful at the masters distance of 1000 m a high VO_2 max is crucial. Longer head races, 15-30 minutes, don't require as high a VO_2 max.

1.1.2 Anaerobic Threshold

The body is always producing and using lactate. The rate of production and the rate of removal are normally equal so there is no build up of lactic acid in the blood or muscles. Anaerobic threshold is the point where the rate of production of lactic acid exceeds the rate of removal. This causes a rapid accumulation of lactate in the blood and muscles resulting in fatigue. Normally this occurs around 4mMol (a mMol is the unit of measure for lactate and represents the concentration of lactic acid in a liter of blood)

The speed at anaerobic threshold is the best indicator of rowing performance for head races and small boat 2000 m rowing. In a 2000 m race the middle 4-5 minutes are usually done at a speed that is equal to anaerobic threshold. In a 1000 m race anaerobic threshold is less important than VO_2 max

1.1.3 Aerobic Threshold

Aerobic threshold is the point where anaerobic metabolism first starts to make a contribution to energy production. This usually occurs around 2mMol and is seen as a slow rise in blood lactate levels. While it does not directly correlate to rowing performance exercise below the anaerobic threshold is very important to a rower. Exercise at this intensity is used to build an aerobic base and forms the platform from which other types of training can be launched.

1.1.4 Thresholds and Muscle Fiber Types

	ST	FOG	FTC	FG
Aerobic Capacity	Very High	High	Moderate	Low
Anaerobic Alactic	Low	Moderate	High	Very High
Anaerobic Glyc.	Low	Moderate	High	Very High
Power output	Low	Moderate	High	Very High
Time to fatigue	Very High	High	Moderate	Low
Preferred Fuel	CHO, fat	CHO	CHO	CHO

Table 1: Fiber type characteristics

Depending on the analysis method there are usually three or four distinct types of muscle fibers. Their characteristics can be seen in Table 1. While the general population has about equal numbers of slow twitch fibers and fast twitch fibers, rowers have a much larger proportion of slow twitch fibers. These slow twitch fibers are capable of using lactic acid as a fuel source. In other words, efficient, fit, slow twitch fibers will eat up the lactic acid that your fast fibers are producing. This helps to decrease the impact of lactic acid on performance such as fatigue, decreased skill, pain in the muscles, and difficulty concentrating on rowing.

During exercise your body activates muscle fibers according to the size principal. The size principal states that motor units are activated from the smallest to the largest as intensity of exercise increases. Slow twitch fibers tend to be in the smallest motor units and are activated at lower intensities. Once the thresholds are determined training categories can be developed that allow a rower to target specific muscle fiber types, increasing the accuracy and effectiveness of the training program.

1.2 Aerobic Training Categories

There are five aerobic and one anaerobic training categories. Each of the categories causes a specific adaptation that moves you one step closer to achieving your performance goals. Over the course of a training year the categories are performed in the order presented. When a higher category is introduced the lower category is maintained.

1.2.1 Category VI

Category VI (CAT VI) encompasses all intensities up to aerobic threshold. Slow twitch muscle fibers are targeted during category VI training leading to improved lactic acid removal and rowing efficiency. Aerobic base, built doing category VI work, is the foundation for higher intensity interval training. During the work phase of an interval lactic acid builds up. If the lactate is not removed during the recovery phase of the interval the next work period will not be done at the same speed as the previous one. In order for intervals to be effective the speed of each interval must be maintained. Without an adequate base, a high volume of interval training is impossible.

CAT. VI	
Time/Session	45 min-2 hours
Sessions/Week	3-8
Sessions/Day	1-3
Style	Continuous steady state
Maintenance	2-3/wk

Sample Workouts:

- 60 minutes steady state. Rate 22-24
- 3 x 30 minutes with 5 minutes rest between. Rate 20-22
- 5 x 15 minutes no rest. Rate 20,22,24,22,20

The majority of the year is spent training in category VI. There have been several studies that have looked at the training programs used by the top rowing countries in the world. They have consistently found that the top rowers perform only 5-10% of their total training volume as higher intensity intervals. Increasing the volume of these intervals doesn't seem to increase VO_2 max or rowing performance any more than the lower volume. In fact many countries have their athletes spend more than 80% of their training time below aerobic threshold.

Category VI training is not only preparation for interval training but is the ideal intensity for technical work. Skill learning is most effective at lower intensities because of low levels of fatigue. Lactic acid and fatigue impairs the ability to learn skills. It is only following 5000 repetitions done exactly the same way at low speed that a skill becomes automated; then the skill can be successfully transferred to higher intensity training and performance.

When designing exercise prescriptions for category VI several key concepts should be remembered: (1) Long training sessions are done less frequently. For example, 4-hour training sessions need only be done 2 to 3 times per week but 60 minute sessions may be done 8 to 10 times per week. (2) The duration of the training session should, in part, be based on the demands of the event. In a sport such as cycling, where the race can last as long as 4 hours, long training sessions are needed to simulate the event. Rowing races vary from 4-30 minutes, so 45-minute sessions are often all that is needed. Sessions less than 45 minutes are not long enough to create a training effect. (3) During certain phases of the year training will be focused on specific event preparation. During this time category VI training should be maintained so that detraining does not occur. (4) Maintenance refers to the number of sessions per week that need to be done to prevent detraining. (5) If the training session is less than two hours long, another category VI session could be done with 2 to 4 hours rest.

1.2.2 Category V

CAT. V	
Time/Session	45 min-2 hours
Sessions/Week	2-5
Sessions/Day	1-3
Style	Continuous steady state
Maintenance	2-3/wk

Category V (CAT V) represents those training intensities between aerobic threshold and anaerobic threshold. Category V is part of aerobic base training. Since category V is between the thresholds the lactate values for this category fall between two and four mMol of lactate.

Sample Workouts:

- 60 minutes steady state. Rate 24-26
- 2 x 30 minutes with 5 minutes rest between. Rate 20-22
- 10 x 5 minutes no rest. Rate 18-24 change every 5 minutes

CAT V training is important for head racing. In longer head races, 30 minutes or more, as much as half of the race may be done at the upper end of category V. No more than 3-5% of total training volume should be dedicated to category V. This number can increase to 10% if several years of high volume category VI training have firmly established aerobic base. Those who race 1000 m races will only use category V training occasionally to add variety to a program.

Category V training uses ST fibers as well as some FOG (fast oxidative glycolytic) fibers. FOG fibers are an endurance fast twitch fiber with as much or more aerobic capacity than slow twitch fibers. In rowers, the FOG fibers are the largest fibers but are not as plentiful as the slow twitch fibers.

Training in category V can be done either as steady-state exercise or long undulating intervals. Since category V intervals are below anaerobic threshold they do not cause an accumulation of lactic acid. Therefore, there are no set work and rest periods. The main purpose of the intervals is to vary the motor units that are recruited by changing exercise intensity. Since the intensity is only slightly higher training volumes tend to be similar to category VI.

Category V training is usually started after 6 to 8 weeks of category VI training are completed. Introduce category V gradually by replacing one category VI session per week with a category V session. The key concepts outlined in category VI apply to category V. Category V sessions rely primarily on carbohydrate as an energy source. In order to replenish the carbohydrate used the time between category V sessions should be 8 to 12 hours. When category V training is started there may be a reduction in the number of category VI sessions.

1.2.3 Category IV

CAT. IV	
Time/Session	30-90 min
Sessions/Week	1-5
Sessions/Day	1-2
Style	Interval or Steady state
Work time	5-10 min
Rest time	5-10 min
Maintenance	1/wk

Category IV (CAT IV) is a narrow band just above and just below anaerobic threshold. Lactate values for category IV fall between 3.5 and 5.5 mMol. There are two objectives to category IV training. For those racing 1000 and 2000 m the goal is to move anaerobic threshold closer to VO_2 max. Ideally anaerobic threshold occurs at 80-85% of VO_2 max. Interval training can be used to increase anaerobic threshold.

Sample Workouts:
- 4 x 12 minutes. Rate 20,26,20,26
- 2 x 20 minutes at head race pace
- 10 x 5 minutes. 5% faster than AT, 5% slower than AT

Most training at or above anaerobic threshold uses intervals. The volume of high intensity work is the key to improvement in these categories. The recovery period between intervals lets the body deal with the lactate that is produced during the work period. This allows a higher volume to be completed than if no recovery periods were taken. Recovery periods for aerobic training should not be less than 3-5 minutes. Using a 2-3:1 rest:work ratio will ensure adequate recovery between repeats. In other words, if your work interval is 3 minutes the recovery interval is 6-9 minutes. Recovery should be active in either category VI or V.

One of the goals of preparing for a head race is to increase the amount of time that anaerobic threshold can be maintained. Threshold endurance training uses steady state exercise at anaerobic threshold for periods of 20-30 minutes. These training sessions become very similar to races and should only be done in the 4-6 weeks prior to the racing season. Training for threshold endurance more than once a week can quickly lead to overtraining and possible injury. Intervals can be done more often.

1.2.4 Category III
Category III represents intensities between anaerobic threshold and VO_2 max. Since category III is above anaerobic threshold, training has to be done interval style to obtain an adequate volume. One of the objectives of category III training is to let the athlete perform at higher levels of lactate and to promote lactate recovery. Many of the cardiac adaptations to aerobic training are seen at this training category. Since the intensity of category III training is quite high no more than 1-2 training sessions per week of this training should be scheduled.

Normally, category III is trained during the pre-competitive and competitive phases of the year with occasional maintenance sessions (once a month) during the rest of the year. More than 4 to 6 weeks of category III training is unnecessary and doesn't produce better fitness. The increase in peak power

CAT. III	
Time/Session	30-90 min
Sessions/Week	1-3
Sessions/Day	1
Style	Interval
Work time	4-10 min
Rest time	8-20 min
Maintenance	1/wk during racing season

Sample Workouts:

• 4 x 750m at just below race pace with 10 min CAT VI between
•2 x 1500 m, rate 28-30 with 12 min CAT VI between

output following category III training is a good indicator of increased VO_2 max. Category III intervals are 4 to 10 minutes duration with 8 to 20 minutes recovery. Recovery is active and is done in category VI. This is repeated for a total of 20 to 30 minutes of work time per training session.

1.2.5 Category II

Category II training is where the participants perform for as long as possible at VO_2 max. The objective of category II training is to increase VO_2 max and endurance time at VO_2 max. VO_2 max level exercise can normally be maintained for 2 to 12 minutes with an average of 6 minutes. In preparing for a 1000 m race category II training should be done once a week for the final month before a major competition. However, if racing frequently, more than twice a month, category II training is unnecessary.

Training in category II is similar to category III. Intervals consist of 2 to 7 minutes work followed by 10 to 20 minutes rest. This is repeated for a total of 10 to 20 minutes of work per training session. Since the intensity is very high,

CAT. II	
Time/Session	30-90 min
Sessions/Week	1-2
Sessions/Day	1
Style	Interval
Work time	2-7 min
Rest time	10-20 min
Maintenance	racing

Sample Workouts:
- 3 x 1000 m at race pace
- 5 x 500 m at race pace

this type of training should only be done 1 to 2 times per week and only during the final part of the pre-competitive phase. Regular racing is often enough to maintain and even improve category II fitness.

1.2.6 Category I

Category I is an anaerobic training category. Humans produce energy from two energy systems. The aerobic system requires oxygen to take part in the chemical reactions that produce energy. The anaerobic energy systems don't require oxygen. The anaerobic systems produce energy at a much higher rate than the aerobic system but they have a limited capacity. In 2000 m racing about 70-80% of the energy used comes from the aerobic system and 20-30% from the anaerobic systems. A 1000 m race which takes about 3:30-4:30 to complete is probably about 50-60% anaerobic and 40-50% aerobic.

Anaerobic training, consisting of all-out sprints for 10 seconds-2 minutes, plays a more important role for a masters rower. Energy for the initial 20 seconds of the race is provided by the anaerobic alactic energy system. This means that the body is using the energy (ATP-CP) that is stored in the muscles for immediate use. Improvements in this system can be brought about either through training or by using a creatine supplement. While using a creatine supplement is the fast way to increase the capacity of the anaerobic alactic system it may result in water retention and weight gain, which may offset any performance improvement the supplement provides. Anaerobic alactic training is done using short sprints of 5-20 seconds in duration. The sprints can be done from a stop or while the boat is moving. These sprints should be added to the program about 6 weeks prior to your major competition 1-2 times per week. They can be used occasionally during winter training but not more than once a month.

The final sprint, with about 300–500 m left in the race, is supported by the anaerobic lactic energy system (anaerobic glycolysis). Accounting for up to 50% of the race, the final sprint is crucial for success in a 1000 m race. Training the anaerobic lactic energy system improves the rate of energy production in this system and increases the body's ability to buffer or tolerate lactic acid. As with the alactic sprints the anaerobic lactic training is introduced 6-8 weeks before the major competition and is done only about once a week. There should be at least one day between anaerobic training sessions. The table below outlines training guidelines for both alactic and lactic training.

	Anaerobic Alactic	Anaerobic Lactic
Work	5-20 seconds	20-120 seconds
Rest	4-6 times the work interval	5-7 times the work interval
Pause	5 minutes	5-10 minutes
Volume per Set	60 seconds work	120 seconds work
Total Volume	5 sets	3-5 sets

Table 2: Anaerobic Training Guidelines

20

- Work refers to the duration of each sprint.
- Rest time is calculated by multiplying the work time by the appropriate number, i.e. a 10 second sprint would require a 40-60 second rest (10 seconds work x 4-6 seconds rest).
- Pause is a period of active rest between each set
- Each set is 60 seconds of work. A 10 second sprint requires 6 repeats per set (60 seconds per set/10 seconds per sprint)

Using training categories adds precision to a training program. To further individualise a program, training categories should be carefully determined.

1.3 Determining Training Categories

The concept of aerobic training categories is only of value if the categories are determined individually for the athlete. Often coaches try to prescribe the same heart rate or wattage range for every athlete without consideration for variations in fitness level or physiological differences. This is done because many rowers don't have the tools or knowledge to determine their categories.

1.3.1 Methods of Determining Training Categories

There are two methods that can be used to determine aerobic training categories. (1) Direct measures involving either gas exchange or blood lactate measures and (2) prediction methods involving the prediction of training categories based on various performance tests. Direct measures are by far the most accurate way to determine the categories but they can be expensive and are not always readily available to individuals or clubs not linked to colleges with human performance laboratories.

Blood Lactate Analysis

With the advent of affordable portable lactate analyzers and mail-order analysis labs, lactate analysis has grown in popularity. Since the training categories have been developed based on lactate levels this is the most accurate method of intensity determination. There are several principles that should be followed for lactate tests to be useful.

- Use a mode of exercise specific to the competitive performance. In other words, rowers need to be tested on the water or on an ergometer. The training zones developed from a bike or treadmill test can't be used for rowing. Conversely, the categories from a rowing-specific test can't be used for running or biking.

- Set the initial workload at or above 30% of VO_2 max. This represents an intensity that is about 30% of 2000 m pace. Starting intensities lower than this are so low that most rowers will not be able to effectively row that easily and results will be artificially high.

- Employ work-load increments of at least 3 minutes duration. Different countries use different stage lengths during lactate testing. Typically, stages will vary from 3 to 5 minutes but stages of up to 8 minutes have been tried in several countries.

- Use the fingertip or earlobe for sampling of capillary blood. There may be some differences in lactate levels due to sampling site. The most important factor is consistency. Every test should employ the same sampling technique.

- Results should be reported in terms of the individual's response to exercise. Thresholds and training categories should be developed using both heart rate and wattage (split time) ranges.

Pre-Test Procedure

The training and nutritional regimens two days prior to the testing session can have an impact on the results. The following guidelines should be followed prior to each testing session. This will help ensure accuracy in test administration and data interpretation.

Maintain a High-carbohydrate Diet

Try to emphasize foods such as pasta, rice, bread, and potatoes in your meals. Some type of carbohydrate drink (gatorade, power-ade, exceed, etc.) should be consumed immediately (within 30 minutes) following your workouts. Fat and protein will have no effect on lactate levels, but may detract from the amount of carbohydrate consumed. Avoid all alcohol.

Caffeine Raises Both Lactate and Heart Rate Levels

Do not consume caffeinated beverages in the 90-minute period before the test. If you have a morning test and are a habitual caffeine user you should try to consume your caffeine early enough so that it will not affect the test results.

Avoid Higher Intensity Training

Strength training and categories V, IV, and III all use carbohydrates as their major fuel source. Carbohydrate depletion will result in false results. If you are training during the two days prior to testing try to do only category VI, and technical sessions. Use some form of carbohydrate drink during these sessions and try to keep them to 90 minutes or less. Only one training session should be done the day before the test.

The Test

The test is a progressive, incremental, discontinuous, submaximal test. Each stage is 3 to 5 minutes long, wattages are increased each stage, the wattages used are determined by your category and gender (i.e. lightweight or heavyweight, male or female). 1 minute of rest is given between each stage during which lactate samples are taken from the fingertip or earlobe.

Warm-up

Your warm-up should be standardized and consistent from test to test. The warm-up should be of sufficient duration to increase temperature but not so long as to decrease intramuscular glycogen levels. 10 to 15 minutes of rowing at an intensity slightly below or equal to the intensity of the first stage of the test is usually sufficient. Have a drink of water before the test starts. There should be no more than 10 minutes between the end of the warm-up and the start of the test.

Stroke Rate

There doesn't seem to be much consensus on the influence of stroke rate on test results. Some countries allow the athlete to choose a stroke rate that is comfortable to achieve a given wattage. The Canadian system uses a stroke rate that is held constant throughout the test and falls between 22 and 26 strokes per minute. More work needs to be done to determine how much of an effect stroke rate has on lactate levels.

Test Performance

The average watt reading on the Concept II ergometer is used for this test so the athlete needs to be as consistent as possible during each stage. The athlete should build up to the desired wattage over the first 15 seconds of the stage. Some athletes will try to 'cheat' the test by using a racing start for the first few strokes and then sitting at a lower wattage for the rest of the stage.

Resistance

A variety of resistances (vent setting or drag factor on the Concept II) have been used in lactate testing. It is still unclear as to how much of an effect changing the resistance has on test results. Anecdotal evidence suggests that the lactates may be higher for any given wattage as the resistance increases but this still needs to be formally investigated.

Stage	HW Men	HW Women	LW Men	LW Women
1	260	160	190	140
2	295	190	230	170
3	330	220	270	200
4	365	250	310	230
5	400	280	350	260
6	435	310	390	290

Table 3: Lactate Test Wattage for National Level Rowers

Stage	HW Men	HW Women	LW Men	LW Women
1	185	125	150	100
2	215	155	180	130
3	245	185	210	160
4	275	215	240	190
5	305	245	270	220
6	335	275	300	250

Table 4: Lactate Test Wattages for Intermediate Rowers

Stage	HW Men	HW Women	LW Men	LW Women
1	150	100	125	75
2	180	130	155	105
3	210	160	185	135
4	240	190	215	165
5	270	220	245	195
6	300	250	275	225

Table 5: Lactate Test Wattages for Recreational Rowers

Note: The level of performance in masters athletes can vary depending on experience and the competitive nature of the individual and club. These wattages should serve as a starting point but may have to be modified to accommodate higher level masters competitors

Wattage

The wattage for each stage and the number of stages will depend on the level of the athlete and the finances available for the testing (more stages usually cost more). At least four stages are needed to develop a graph from which the training categories can be developed. If the number of stages have to be limited because of time or money constraints, it is more important to have stages below anaerobic threshold than above anaerobic threshold. This will allow the development of categories VI through IV which should comprise the majority of training time. Tables 3 to 5 provide some suggested wattages for various performance levels. These wattages are not the only possible ranges but have been found to provide lactate levels appropriate for the determination of all training categories.

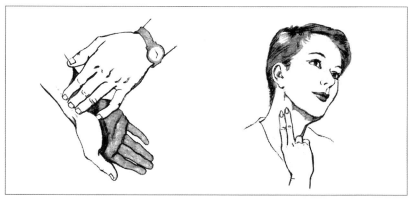

Heart Rate can either be palpated at the wrist or the neck. Be careful not to press too hard or the pulse won't be felt.

As a final word of caution: Although the technology is available for coaches or athletes to perform a lactate analysis, all lactate testing should be done by an experienced technician. There is a certain amount of skill involved in taking and analyzing blood samples. If self-testing is done, be prepared to get inaccurate results until sampling skills have been developed.

Maximal Heart Rate Methods

Many coaches rely on percentages of maximal heart rate as a means of estimating thresholds and training zones. The use of heart rate to determine exercise intensity is possible because there is a relatively linear relationship between heart rate and oxygen consumption. This relationship exists for most continuous rhythmical exercises. However, the relationship, though linear, is not the same for all exercises. In other words using 70% of maximum heart rate for erging and treadmill running may induce different training responses. This makes the use of heart rate as the sole indicator of exercise intensity difficult when training for very specific adaptations such as those needed by athletes. However, since health adaptations can occur over a wide variety of exercise intensities, heart rate can be used to set upper and lower limits of exercise intensity for recreational rowing.

Determination of Heart Rate

Before the discussion of heart rate and exercise intensity can be continued, methods of measuring heart rate should be discussed. There are several acceptable methods for measuring heart rate: pulse palpation, ECG, stethoscope, and heart rate monitor. Each has advantages and disadvantages.

Palpation

Palpation involves manually feeling for a pulse rate either at the wrist or at the neck. This is a simple technique with no cost. However, since heart rate is typically counted for 6, 10, or 15 seconds and multiplied to a 1-minute value the amount of error can be quite high. In addition, at very high heart rates or while moving, it is difficult to get an accurate count. Palpation is an acceptable means of determining if someone is within a large heart rate range but is not a good way to find a narrow or precise heart rate range during exercise.

Stethoscope

Placing a stethoscope to the chest and counting the heart beats is an alternative to palpation. Again, the heart rate is normally counted for 6 to 15 seconds and multiplied to a 1-minute value. The stethoscope shares the same problems and limitations as palpation.

ECG

An electrocardiograph measures the electrical activity of the heart during the different phases of a beat. The ECG is very accurate at all heart rates and can be used to indicate existing or potential cardiac abnormalities. While the accuracy and value of ECG is unquestionable, the expense and need to have a physician to interpret the readings make it impractical for everyday use.

Heart-Rate Monitors

Category	% Max HR
VI	60-70
V	70-80
IV	80-90
III	90-100

Heart-rate monitors that include a chest strap and a receiver, usually in the form of a watch, offer the same accuracy as an ECG. Monitors can cost $75 to $300 depending on the features. Displays are normally updated every five seconds. If narrow heart-rate ranges or precise measurement is required, a heart-rate monitor is the most economical tool.

Table 6: Heart Rate Percentages for Aerobic Training Categories

	Lower Limit	Upper Limit
Maximum HR	200	200
Resting HR	- 72	-72
	128	128
% Maximum HR	x.60	x.70
	77	90
Resting HR	+72	+ 72
Target HR	149	162

Table 7: Heart Rate Reserve Method for Calculating Training Categories

Determination of Heart Rate Ranges

Two methods are commonly used to determine heart rate ranges. The first method is to use fixed percentages of maximal heart rate. Rough averages for the heart rate percentages for the different categories can be seen in Table 6. This is the least accurate method of heart rate training and basically amounts to nothing more than a rough guess. This method may be acceptable for people in a 'Learn-to-row' program but will probably result in very poor estimates for more fit individuals.

The second method is called the heart rate reserve method. With this method percentages of the difference between maximum and resting heart rate are used to determine a heart rate range. Research shows that 60 to 80% of heart rate reserve is equal to 60 to 80% VO_2 max. We also know that in untrained people anaerobic threshold (AT) occurs at about 70% VO_2 max. In moderately trained people AT is approximately 80 to 85% VO_2 max and in highly trained rowers AT will be 87 to 92% VO_2 max. Aerobic threshold will fall between 50 to 60% of VO_2 max for untrained, 60 to 70% for moderately trained and 70 to 80% for highly trained individuals. The calculation of the heart rate range for category VI for a moderately trained athlete with maximum heart rate of 200 and resting heart rate of 72 is seen in Table 7.

Maximum Heart Rate

All of the methods presented for determining heart rate training zones are based on percentages of maximum oxygen consumption or maximum heart rate. Maximum heart rate can be determined in two ways. Maximum heart rate can be estimated using the formula (220-age). This formula is only an estimate of maximum heart rate and has an error range of plus or minus 13 beats per minute. This type of error may be acceptable when dealing with individuals who are training to improve health. When more specific goals are established maximum heart rate should be determined directly. An all-out 1000 m sprint will cause heart rate to reach max by the end of the piece.

Heart rate methods are the simplest but least reliable and accurate ways of determining training categories. They don't take into account performance level or the physiological variables that create thresholds. Heart rate has several weaknesses that need to be considered before it can be used as a tool in monitoring training intensity.

Even though there is a relationship between exercise intensity and heart rate this relationship is different for different exercises, i.e. heart rates for running will not be the same as heart rates for rowing for any given intensity. In fact, heart rates for erging and rowing are not the same. Some research indicates that heart rates on the water can be as much as 10 beats higher than on an ergometer for the same oxygen consumption. There is also evidence that rowers who train on water year round have 'on-water' heart rates lower than on the ergometer.

Heart rate is influenced by many variables. Duration of training, emotional stress, clothing, heat, dehydration, overtraining, loss of sleep, decreased blood volume, altitude, and detraining all change the heart-rate response. During long duration steady-state training sessions of 60 minutes or more the heat produced by the body can increase heart rate by as much as 20 beats per minute. If you were to slow down to try to keep your heart rate the same, you would change the training effect for the muscles. During steady-state training the boat speed or power output should remain constant throughout the session regardless of increases in heart rate.

Training in a hot environment can increase heart rate by up to 13 beats per minute. This can make the accurate use of heart rate very difficult. Late in a training cycle heart rates can be different than what they were a week earlier for the same power output. Whether this is higher or lower is difficult to predict. Emotional stress at work or family stress tends to increase heart rate during training. In addition, these types of stress decrease quality of sleep which further increases heart rate. When training in hot weather or during periods of high stress use feelings of fatigue and comfort as a training guide rather than heart rate.

Heart rate is an individual response as is maximum heart rate. For example, people in the same boat may have 20 to 30 beat differences in heart rates during the same training session. This isn't necessarily due to differences in fitness rather it is something inherent to those people. Comparing heart rates with others is unnecessary and often unwise. Training programs should not be based on general heart-rate guidelines, but should be based on individual responses. A training heart rate of 150 bpm may elicit very different adaptations for different people.

Heart rate is not a good tool for monitoring intensity during speed work or interval training. Some coaches believe heart rate should be used to monitor

Using the average 500 m splits from a 20 minute test

Category III is 2 seconds faster

Category IV is 2 seconds slower

Category V is 8 seconds slower

Category VI is 13 seconds slower

Example: If the athlete rows 6000 m in 20 minutes the average split/500 m would be 1:40 therefore:

Category III is 1:38

Category IV is 1:42

Category V is1:48

Category VI is 1:53

Table 8: Split Prediction for Aerobic Traininig Categories

recovery between intervals so fatigue levels can be controlled. While it is true that fatigue levels need to be controlled, heart rate is not the way to do it. The fatigue during high-intensity rowing is caused primarily by lactic acid accumulation. The time between intervals should be based on the time needed to reduce lactate levels. The relationship between heart rate recovery and lactate recovery is not very strong. In other words, heart rate may have recovered but the lactate levels may still be too high to do the interval the way it should be done.

Heart rate is a tool for training. Like all tools it has limitations and should be used for a specific job at a specific time. Boat speed or power output on the ergometer are influenced by fewer factors than heart rate, and may prove to be better indicators of training intensity. If you are going to use heart rate to monitor your intensity follow the guidelines outlined here and remember that heart rate is just a response to internal and external stimuli, it should not be the main controlling factor for your training.

Field/Performance Testing

Using a performance or field test to predict the training categories relies on the relationship between the time to fatigue and aerobic or anaerobic threshold.

Anaerobic threshold has been shown to be an intensity that can be held for 20 to 30 minutes. A 20-minute performance test can be used to estimate the training categories. In the 20-minute test, you are required to row as many meters as possible in 20 minutes.

Dr. Volker Nolte, Canadian lightweight men's coach and a professor at University of Western Ontario, has developed some guidelines for using a 20-minute test to predict categories (Table 8).

Estimates from a performance test to categories can be affected by several factors. Performance tests do not rely only on the physiological capacity of the athlete. A good score on a performance test is a function of physiological, mental, technical, and tactical components working together. There are many athletes who either under or over perform according to their physiological data simply because they did not treat the test like a race and were not properly prepared mentally.

The guidelines in Table 8 are most accurate near anaerobic threshold. The majority of the data used to develop these guidelines used National team calibre athletes. They tend to overestimate category VI in lower level athletes. This is probably because national level athletes have spent more training time in category VI and understand how a category VI session feels. Most lower level athletes, when attempting a category VI session, are actually in category V because they have never accurately had categories determined. This leads to fitness increases in category V without much change in category VI causing this category to be lower than expected.

Aerobic training is the cornerstone of rowing performance. Many rowers use the 'row-as-hard-as-possible-all-the-time' philosophy and wonder why they don't make progress. Working at the proper intensity can be the difference between efficient training and not achieving your competitive goals.

Chapter 2: Flexibility Training

2.1 Flexibility and Rowing Performance

Flexibility is defined as the range of motion (ROM) available at a joint. Flexibility is specific to each joint; that is, a person may have a large ROM at the wrist joint in all directions, but a limited ROM in the shoulder. Flexibility is important to athletes for three reasons: Injury prevention, skill development and performance, and power production.

2.1.1 Flexibility and Injury Prevention

The information available on flexibility and injury prevention is inconclusive. Both high and low levels of flexibility may increase the risk of injury. Low flexibility prevents a joint from moving through it's full range. Compensation movements, improper movement patterns, occur as a result and lead to chronic pain in muscles that become overworked.

Very high flexibility often leaves joints unstable and weak. Stretching before exercise does not appear to decrease the rate of injury. However, stretching after training significantly lowers injury rates. Differences in flexibility between the right and left side of the body seem to have the greatest impact on injury development. A difference of more than 5% can increase the risk of injury 25 times. Sweep rowers develop large strength and flexibility differences if they always row the same side.

2.1.2 Flexibility and Skill Development

Consistency of movement is a key factor in skill development. If you cannot achieve the required range of movement for a skill you will not be able to learn the skill. For instance, lunging at the catch may be the result of inadequate flexibility at the knee and hips. In an attempt to row long it is tempting to lunge to compensate for low flexibility. This can lead to a host of other technical problems. It doesn't matter how much coaching or video work is done, the problem can't be fixed until the flexibility problem is fixed. In high level athletes many technical errors are the result of inadequate strength or flexibility.

2.1.3 Flexibility and Power Production

In rowing, power and boat speed can only be increased while the oar is in the water. Greater flexibility allows the oar to be in the water longer. Flexibility is

33

only one part of the power production equation. If you are too flexible, you may overreach and actually decrease power production at the catch. The muscles are at a mechanical disadvantage in an extreme stretched position.

2.2 Types of Flexibility

There are two main types of flexibility known as active and passive. Passive stretching involves an outside source creating the movement. This outside source may be a partner, a machine, momentum or gravity. During passive stretching the athlete may be active. An example of passive stretching occurs when an athlete uses dumbbells to go through a greater range of motion in the bench press than he could with no weight or a barbell. While the athlete is active the stretch is passive because the weight is forcing the athlete through the range of motion, the athlete is not pulling his arms through the full range. There is a slight risk of injury in passive stretching if the motion is pushed too far.

Active stretching involves the individual moving to a position of slight discomfort and holding this position before releasing. Active flexibility is the ROM available when internal muscle forces cause the movement range. If a segment must be moved through a range by the muscles, weakness in those muscles may cause the ROM to be less than what it would be passively.

2.3 Factors Affecting Flexibility

There are a number of factors that influence flexibility. These include joint structure, age, body type, disease or injury, and inactivity. ROM is joint specific; it depends on the structure of the joint. For example, a ball and socket joint, such as the shoulder, has a greater ROM than a uni- or biaxial joint, such as the knee. The joint capsule is said to account for 47% of a joint's total resistance to movement.

The more active an individual, the greater ROM that individual has. In inactive people, the connective tissue shortens with disuse and restricts the joint's movement. The areas of the body in which large movements of the limbs are neglected, because normal daily activity does not require them, will have the greatest inflexibility. This is not a permanent situation and can be improved by following flexibility or stretching programs. Habitual movement patterns of an

individual are also important. The joint and surrounding tissues adapt to the same movements. Using the joints and muscles in the same activity pattern or maintaining habitual body postures decreases flexibility by causing the muscles to shorten. Stretching the lower back, hips and shoulders is essential for a rower to prevent the back injuries that often occur from constant use during the rowing stroke.

Gender plays a role in flexibility. Women have greater flexibility than men. The female is designed this way, especially in the pelvic region to assist in pregnancy and childbirth. Women tend to have lighter and smaller bone composition that allows greater movement. Women also tend to have smaller and less-defined muscles, thus allowing freer range of movement. While higher flexibility helps prevent low back and hip problems in women, it can lead to shoulder and knee instability increasing the risk of injury in those joints.

Age is a major contributor in flexibility performance. Stiffness and immobility may result from at least three factors: true aging changes, an increasingly sedentary lifestyle, and unrecognizable disease processes. Muscles have less elasticity and flexibility with age. As one grows older, muscle atrophy (a decrease in muscle mass) also occurs. Muscle fibers are replaced by fatty tissue. These changes are partly responsible for decreased flexibility. The gradual loss of elasticity can't be prevented but it can be slowed through a stretching program. Regular strength training will help prevent atrophy and increased fat levels can be avoided with good nutrition.

A second explanation for decreased flexibility is an inactive lifestyle. Many people become less active with age. However, by increasing activity patterns, flexibility can be improved. With job and family commitments added to their training load many master athletes experience a time crunch and let flexibility training slide. The assumption is that the rowing is going to provide everything that is needed. This is not the case. The addition of 10-15 minutes of flexibility training at home while watching TV or during a lunch break at work will help overcome this time crunch.

For some older individuals, undetected diseases set in. These diseases hinder ROM and may cause discomfort to the individual. An example of this is osteoarthritis, the most common musculoskeletal problem in the elderly. There is therapy available, but the results are not guaranteed. A lifetime of physical activity or competitive sport can lead to a variety of joint aches and degeneration. Previous injuries, that seemed minor at the time, and have never been properly rehabilitated are common among master athletes. This is particularly true for activities that cause muscle soreness and an accumulation of scar tissue which is very inflexible.

Body type, in this instance, refers to tendons, ligaments, muscle fascia, skin, and other connective tissues. Bone, muscle, ligament and joint capsule, tendon, and skin determine the range of motion for any joint. Tendons and ligaments provide 10% of the total resistance experienced by a joint during movement. Muscle and its fascia, a protective sheath around the muscle, account for 41% and skin accounts for 2%. Muscle and facia are composed of more elastic tissue and are therefore better in reducing resistance to movement and increasing dynamic flexibility. However, excess fatty tissues and large, hypertrophied muscles may hinder movement. Collagen, fibrous connective tissue, and elastin, elastic tissue, are also determinants. The dominating tissue in a joint area helps in determining its relative ROM. The elastic tissues give greater flexibility as compared to the fibrous tissue.

Because connective tissue is the target for flexibility programs, understanding the response of connective tissue to stretching, or elongation, is important. When connective tissue is elongated, its lengthening has two components: elastic stretching (i.e. it will recoil) and plastic stretching (i.e. it will not recoil). The permanence of the stretch depends on how much plastic stretch occurs; the elastic-type lengthening merely causes recoil of the tissue to its original length. Plastic elongation is directed toward the viscous (thick fluid) property of connective tissue. The contribution of each kind of elongation to the flexibility of the joint depends on how the stretching is performed. The amount of stretching force, the duration of the stretching force, and tissue temperature combine to determine if the stretch is elastic or plastic. Permanent lengthening of connective tissue is produced best by lower force of longer duration applied at elevated tissue temperatures (40°C or 104°F and above in therapeutic settings). Cooling the tissue (by ice packs about 15 min) before releasing the tension seems to increase the permanence of the elongation. In addition, under these conditions, any structural weakening of the tissues is minimized. Elastic lengthening (elongation that will recoil) is produced by high-force, short duration stretching at normal or colder tissue temperatures.

2.4 Stretching Methods

Stretching methods are categorized as static or dynamic. Static stretching is also known as passive or slow, sustained stretching. Dynamic stretching is called active ballistic, bouncing, or fast stretching. Research studies on flexibility improvement indicate that both methods are effective but that static methods are safer and result in less muscle soreness.

2.4.1 Dynamic Stretching

Dynamic stretch of a muscle group brings into play neuromuscular mechanisms involving the muscle spindle (myotatic, or stretch reflex) and the Golgi tendon organ. In fast stretching, the momentum of the moving body segment, rather than an external force, is used to push the articulation beyond its present ROM. Dynamic stretching is important for sports requiring high speed running, jumping, throwing, or striking movements. For example, in baseball, a pitcher's throwing arm is stretched beyond its active range of motion by the momentum generated through the hips and trunk. Training ballistically is the most sport-specific way of improving shoulder flexibility for these athletes. The speed of stretch caused by the dynamic method stimulates the muscle spindles, and the stretch reflex causes a contraction of the same muscles that are being stretched. The greater the speed of muscle stretching, the greater the stretch reflex. Therefore, even though the momentum brings the joint beyond its normal range, the ballistic method causes a countercontraction during the stretch and reduces the training effect. Reports associate muscle soreness with this type of stretching; that is, before motion stops, the sudden tension put on the tissues can result in small tears in the connective tissue or muscle fibers, which leads to swelling or pain. This is very similar to what happens during plyometric training. Since there is no plyometric component to the rowing stroke (even the transition from recovery to catch is too slow to be plyometric) dynamic flexibility is not necessary for rowers.

2.4.2 Static Stretching

Static stretching is the most common form of stretching. It involves assuming a stretched position and holding it for a period of time. Some muscle-spindle activity results from the stretched position, but it is minimal because the spindles react more to the speed of stretch than to the stretched position.

Static, or long duration low force, stretching methods are safer alternatives to ballistic stretching (unless ballistic stretching is sport-specific). In addition, an easy muscle warm-up activity prior to stretching increases the plastic elongation of the tissues due to the increase in temperature. Static stretching exercises should not be done at the beginning of a warm-up routine. Stretching should be performed immediately after the main part of a workout because it is then that the tissue temperatures are the highest. There is some current research suggesting that, in speed and power sports, static stretching should be avoided during the warm-up. Static stretching has been shown to decrease strength by up to 7% in the immediate post-stretch period.

2.4.3 Proprioceptive Neuromuscular Facilitation

The proprioceptive neuromuscular facilitation (PNF) method of stretching in various forms is gaining popularity. Reports indicate that the flexibility of a joint can be increased quickly by this method and little soreness occurs. PNF stretching involves a passive movement to the onset of stretch followed by a maximal isometric contraction against resistance before moving further into the range of motion. The contraction is held for 4-10 seconds followed by 4-10 seconds of relaxation before moving.

PNF training can be done alone or with the aid of a partner. Because PNF exercise is potentially dangerous, especially when performed improperly, communication between the subject and the partner is essential. In order to keep PNF stretching safe the following guidelines for communication should be followed:

- The person being stretched (the subject) is in charge and controls how much they are to be stretched. The person doing the stretching (the partner) should maintain a strong stable body position. This will prevent slipping or falling when the contraction is performed.
- The partner must insure that joints are properly aligned. Forceful contractions in poorly aligned joints can lead to injuries.
- The subject should tell the partner when beginning the contraction.
- The partner acts as an object that the subject pushes against. The partner should never push against the subject.
- The partner should immediately remove all stretch from the subject if they are told to.
- When trying to increase the range of motion following the contraction do so slowly.
- The subject should increase the force of the contraction slowly.
- Starting with a maximal contraction can throw the partner off balance.
- Try to relax the muscles surrounding the joint during the stretch.

2.5 Planning a Flexibility Program

Choosing a Stretch

The decision as to what stretches should be done must be based on an analysis of the athlete. Technical errors need to be analyzed to determine if they are caused by flexibility problems. Body symmetry should be tested to determine if there is a flexibility imbalance between the right and left sides. Flexibility training should only be done for joints that are inflexible. Improving flexibility in an already flexible joint may create an instability and increase the chance of injury. The exercises at the end of this chapter target specific problem areas for most rowers. If any stretch hurts remove it from the program and try to find the cause of the pain.

Choosing a Method

The type of stretching used (static, ballistic, PNF) depends on the demands of the sport. In a sport like rowing either static or PNF would be appropriate since there are no ballistic movements in the sport. In wrestling, PNF is more appropriate since the athlete is often isometrically contracting their muscles while under extreme stretch. For sprinters, ballistic flexibility would be most important through the ankles and hips. Each type of stretching has value in specific circumstances. PNF and ballistic stretching should not be dismissed as dangerous forms of exercise because of biases developed by the fitness industry geared towards sedentary, untrained people.

Frequency of Stretching

If the stretching program is not overly aggressive, stretching can be done every day. Ballistic stretching and PNF sometimes result in muscle or joint soreness the day after the session. If this is occurring you should wait 3-4 days before the next stretching session.

Duration of Stretch

There has been quite a bit of debate over how long a stretch should be held. Currently it is believed that the most important factor is the total stretch time and not the duration of a single stretch. In order to most effectively improve flexibility a total of 60 seconds of stretch time needs to be done for each movement in the program. For instance 3 stretches of 20 seconds each produces a total stretch time of 60 seconds. 6 stretches for 10 seconds each also produces a total stretch time of 60 seconds.

When to Stretch

Stretching during a warm-up does not prevent injury nor does it increase flexibility. Static stretching during a warm-up may even decrease performance in strength and power activities. Stretching during a warm-up is primarily to help establish the existing range of motion and enhance technical skills. To improve flexibility stretching should be done after a training session. When muscle temperatures are high the muscles are more elastic and receptive to stretching.

2.6 Stretching Exercises

The following stretching exercises have been included because they address the specific needs of rowers. Doing all the stretches will ensure a balanced effective program. Follow the order that they are listed. Remember to stretch only after a training session when the muscles are warm and more elastic.

Ankle Stretch

- Sit upright on the floor or a chair with one leg crossed over the other.
- Hold the bent leg just above the ankle with one hand and hold the foot with the other.
- Pull the foot towards the body and hold.
- Pull the foot away from the body and hold.
- Bend the ankle to one side and hold.
- This stretch should be felt in the ankles, shins, and calves.

Triangle Stretch

- From a push up position move the hands towards the feet in order to raise the hips and form a triangle.
- At the peak of the triangle force the heels onto the ground (this can be done both legs at once or one leg at a time as in the picture).
- This stretch should be felt in the calves, hamstrings, and achilles tendon.

Step Calf Stretch

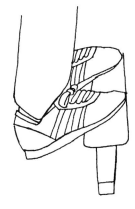

- Stand with the balls of the feet balanced on the edge of a step.
- Slowly lower the heels as far as possible.
- This stretch should be felt in the calves and achilles tendon.

Wall Calf Stretch

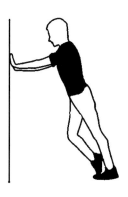

- Stand arms length away from a wall.
- Step forward slightly with one leg while keeping the other leg straight.
- Keeping the body straight shift the body weight forward and lean against the wall.
- Make sure to keep the rear foot down and in line with the hips.
- This stretch should be felt in the calves, and hamstrings.

Sit and Reach

- Sit upright with both legs extended.
- Keeping both legs straight bend from the waist and lower the torso against the thighs.
- This stretch should be felt in the hamstrings of both legs and lower back.

Inner Thigh Stretch

- Sit upright on the floor.
- Bend the knees, bring the heels together, pull the feet towards the buttocks.
- Place the hands or elbows on the inside of the thighs just above the knees.
- Slowly push the knees towards the floor.
- This stretch should be felt along the inside of the thighs.

43

Stride Stretch

- Stand upright with feet together.
- Step forward as far as possible with one leg while keeping the other stationary.
- Keep the front foot pointing straight ahead.
- Slowly force the back thigh towards the floor.
- This stretch should be felt in the hip flexors and quads of the back leg.

Glute Stretch

- Lie flat on your back.
- Raise one leg straight up and bend the knee to 90°.
- Hold the leg by placing the hands behind the knee.
- Pull the knee towards the chest.
- Keep the upper body flat on the floor.
- This stretch should be felt in the buttocks.

Standing Quad Stretch

- Standing upright hold onto something for support.
- Bend one leg so that the heel approaches the buttocks.
- Grab the leg with the hand on the same side of the body and pull the heel closer to the buttocks.
- This stretch should be felt in the quadriceps.

Lying Quad Stretch

- Lie on your side, keep your body straight.
- Bend one leg so that the heel approaches the buttocks.
- Grab the leg with the hand on the same side of the body and pull the heel closer to the buttocks.
- This stretch should be felt in the quadriceps.

45

Lying Hip Stretch

- Lie flat on your back.
- Raise one leg straight up.
- Hold on to the knee or thigh with one hand.
- Pull the knee across the body towards the floor.
- Keep the upper body flat on the floor.
- This stretch should be felt in the lower back and hips.

Abdominal Stretch

- Kneel on the floor looking straight ahead.
- Reach back and place your hands on your heels.
- Lean back onto your hands keeping your legs straight.
- Look back to increase the stretch.
- This stretch should be felt through the abdominals.

Twisting Stretch

- Sit on the floor.
- Keeping the hips facing forward twist to one side.
- This stretch should be felt in the abdominals and lower back.
- Do not use the floor to force yourself into a stretched position. Only stretch as far as you can without assistance from the floor.

Wall Shoulder Stretch

- Stand in a doorway or near a wall.
- Raise the arms overhead.
- Bend at the waist and place your arms against a wall or doorway.
- Gently pull down with the arms.
- This stretch should be felt in the upper back and under the arms.

Side Bend

- Sit on the floor with the trunk upright and legs apart.
- Raise one hand overhead.
- Bend from the waist towards one side.
- This stretch should be felt along the sides and abdominals.

Rear Shoulder Stretch

- Stand upright feet shoulder-width apart.
- Raise one arm to the front at shoulder height.
- Hold the extended arm at the elbow and pull it across the body.
- This stretch should be felt in the back of the shoulder and tricep.

48

Forearm and Wrist Stretch

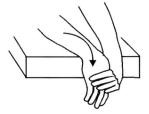

- Place your forearm on a table palm down with your wrist over the edge.
- Gently push down on the top of the hand.
- Turn the arm over so the palm is up and gently push down on the fingers.
- Grasp the hand just above the wrist.
- Keeping the fingers straight pull the hand to the left and then to the right.

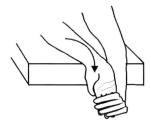

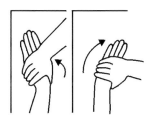

Chapter 3: Strength Training

Strength is a crucial part of the development of a rower. This is particularly true for the masters rower. Strength becomes much more important for a 1000 m race than a 2000 m race. Strength in rowing is most important for the start phase of the race which can last 15-20 seconds. In a 2000 m race the start accounts for about 4% of the total race time. In the 1000 m race the start accounts for just over 8% of the race. This means that a competitor has less time to overcome a poor start in the 1000 m race. Not only will strength training improve power and performance at the start of the race it helps prevent injury and can improve balance and coordination which improves technique.

3.1 Strength Training Concepts

Muscle Actions

A muscle action refers to the state of activity of a muscle. Muscles are capable of three types of activity:

- Concentric muscle actions involve the shortening of the muscle and are usually seen when the body or a weight is lifted. In ski jumping the take-off involves a concentric contraction of the quadriceps muscles (the muscles in the front of the thigh).
- Eccentric muscle actions involve lengthening of a muscle and are usually seen when a weight is being lowered or the body is decelerated. Landings involve an eccentric contraction of the quadriceps muscles.
- Isometric muscle actions involve no change in the length of a muscle. The maintenance of body positions during the in run and while in the air is accomplished through isometric muscle actions.

Sets and Reps

In strength training a movement cycle consists of a concentric and an eccentric contraction. This cycle is known as a repetition or "rep". When several repetitions are performed in a row this is known as a set. The number of sets and repetitions that are performed during a training session depends upon the age and experience of the athlete as well as the goals of the training session.

Intensity and Volume

Intensity is the tension or stress put on the muscle. Intensity is influenced by the number of sets and reps and the rest between sets but mostly intensity is affected by the amount of weight that is being lifted. Intensity is relative, what is intense for one person may be quite easy for another. In order to compensate for the relative nature of intensity it is most often expressed as a % of maximum (1RM).

3.2 Strength Training for Injury Prevention

Strength training can help prevent both acute injuries like strained muscles as well as the chronic aches and pains that occur as a result of years of training. Many of the chronic injuries in rowing occur as the result of muscle imbalances. Muscle imbalances occur when the right and left sides of the body don't have equal strength or when the muscles on the front and back of the body don't have equal strength. Rowing, particularly sweep rowing, causes muscle imbalances. When right and left differences are large the muscles pull unevenly on the bones. This is especially evident around the spine and pelvis. Uneven pulling can result in alignment problems that must then be treated by a chiropractor or medical doctor. Because of the potential medical problems associated with right-left asymmetries a strength program should insure that this problem is corrected or prevented.

Muscle imbalances should be addressed in the early part of the off - season. It is relatively safe to assume that, unless you have tried to eliminate them, that you have some sort of a muscle imbalance. The following procedure is a good way of correcting this problem.

Phase I. Bilateral Phase

Purpose: To re-educate the right and left sides to work together equally and to start strengthening the weak side.

Intensity:	60-70% of maximum
Sets:	2-3 sets
Repetitions:	8-10
Exercises/body part:	1-2
Times/ week:	2-3

The bilateral phase involves exercises where the right and left sides work together and make sure that weight is moving evenly. Technique is extremely important.

Phase II. Alternation Phase

Purpose: To work the right and left sides separately so that greater stability is developed in the weak side.

Intensity:	70-75% of maximum
Sets:	2-3 sets
Repetitions:	6-8
Exercises/body part:	1-2
Times/ week:	2-3

Exercises that work the right and left sides separately are done during this phase (dumbbells are good for this). The same weight and number of repetitions should be used for both sides. Let the weaker side dictate the amount of weight.

Phase III. Accumulation Phase

Purpose: To increase the work volume in order to stimulate muscle growth in the weak side.

Intensity:	70-75% of maximum
Sets:	2-3 sets for strong side, 4-6 for weak side
Repetitions:	6-8
Exercises/body part:	1-2
Times/ week:	2-3

This phase is particularly important for athletes returning to rowing after an injury. Often an injured limb will lose muscle mass as a result of inactivity. To permanently solve the muscle imbalance problem the size of the muscles on both sides of the body have to be equal. Two or three weeks should be spent in each of the phases. After this program is completed you will need to keep some exercises in the program that work the right and left sides independently. This will ensure that the muscle imbalance doesn't come back every year.

3.3 Improving Balance and Stability

Balance and stability can be limiting factors in rowing performance. As you age your balance systems, particularly the visual and inner ear, are among the first to deteriorate. This places a greater load on the muscles for balance and stability. Not only is balance important to keep you in the boat but it can save you energy and make your stroke more efficient.

A rower who is fighting to keep their balance cannot use those muscles to apply power to the oar. Inefficient balance muscles that are working harder are also using energy that should be reserved for boat moving. Training to improve balance and stability involves putting yourself in progressively more off-balance situations.

The Swiss ball is an excellent tool for balance training for rowing. Swiss balls can be used to simulate the seated position in rowing and force the abdominal muscles to act to stabilize the body. These balls can be purchased in most of the large retail stores or sporting good shops.

Check the box to make sure you get the right size. Because most of the stability exercises involve just using body weight it is difficult to prescribe sets and reps for this type of training. Instead, select 3 or 4 exercises and work on them for a total of 20-30 minutes 2 or 3 times per week. Once you have mastered those exercises choose some new ones.

3.4 Improving Strength and Power

3.4.1 Intensity and Volume

	Size	Strength	Max. Strength	Power	Strength Endurance
Sets	3-5	3-5	2-3	3-5	1-5
Reps/set	8-12	4-6	2-3	4-6	30-200
Volume	30-40	20-30	10-15	12-20	150-200
Intensity	60-75%	75-90%	90-100%	70-80%	30-50%
Speed	Moderate	Moderate	Explosive	Explosive	Explosive
Weeks	8-12	4-8	4-8	4-6	4
Cycle	3:1	3:1	2:1	3:1	3:1

Table 9: Volume and Intensity Combinations

Strength is the amount of force that can be produced. Power is a combination of strength and speed. The combination of volume, the number of sets and reps, and the intensity, the percentage of maximum weight used, determines the training effect that you will get. Table 9 shows the combinations of intensity and volume and the result of that combination.

When using this table start on the far left with size training during the start of the off season. Don't worry about gaining huge amounts of muscle mass with this type of size training. The combination of aerobic training and age makes it difficult to gain size. Rowers probably won't gain more than 1-3 pounds per year. Progressively follow the table from left to right for the prescribed number of weeks.

Volume refers to the number of total repetitions per body part. In other words, if you are in the size phase and do three sets of ten squats that would be all the exercises you would do for your legs because you have reached the 30 reps you need. The bottom row labelled cycle refers to the number of work and recovery weeks. Recovery weeks are extremely important. They allow your body to fully adapt to the training it has been doing. Without recovery weeks overtraining is likely to occur. During a recovery week the volume for each body part should be cut in half and the intensity is dropped to 50%.

During the max strength, power, and power endurance phases the speed is explosive. Speed of movement is a very important strength training variable. Strength increases occur only at the speeds used in training. In order for the strength training to transfer to on water performance you need to be as dynamic as possible during these phases. In the max strength phase the weight will be quite heavy so the weight may not seem to be moving fast but the intention to move fast has to be present.

To determine the maximum amount of weight you can lift, so that you can use the appropriate intensity, find a weight you can lift for 2-10 reps. Do as many repetitions as possible with this weight and put the numbers in the formula below.

$$\text{Max} = ((0.033 \times \text{reps}) \times \text{weight lifted}) + \text{weight lifted}$$

You should retest your max at the end of each cycle. This will make sure that you will continue to progress throughout the program.

3.4.2 Rest Between Sets

The amount of rest between sets has been the subject of much debate in popular bodybuilding books. It has often been advocated that rest between sets should be limited to less than 1 minute. The reasoning for this was that by keeping the muscles tired more muscle fibers would have to be activated to do the work. There is no evidence that this is true. In fact, rest periods of this sort will limit the total amount of work that can be done and thereby decrease the effectiveness of the training program. This is because very short rest periods do not allow a complete recovery of the Anaerobic Alactic energy system or time for removal of lactic acid.

Strength training with sets of fewer than 6 repetitions uses predominantly the anaerobic alactic energy system. The alactic energy system relies on the energy stored in the muscles. Energy is stored in the form of ATP and CP. These two compounds, known as the phosphagens, are available for immediate use. The stored supply of these compounds is relatively small, they can provide energy for about 10-15 seconds of all-out effort. Once all the stored energy is used up, the body requires about 3 minutes to fully replace the phosphagens. If the next set is started before the phosphagens are fully restored the muscles will be forced to use the anaerobic lactic energy system. This will result in a build-up of lactic acid.

Lactic acid is responsible for the burning sensation in the muscles. It also causes feelings of heaviness and fatigue. Contrary to popular belief lactic acid does not promote increases in muscular size or strength. In fact, a build-up of lactic acid will inhibit the quantity and quality of work performed resulting in fewer strength and size gains.

Lactic acid, an acidic end product of anaerobic glycolysis, can decrease the ph in the muscle. The enzymes that are responsible for energy production are very sensitive to changes in ph. When the ph drops these enzymes stop functioning and the muscle fibres can no longer produce energy. As a result of the shut down in energy production the muscle fibers is no longer capable of participating in the exercise. When enough muscle fibres drop out of the exercise the weight cannot be lifted anymore. Contrary to what you will read in the popular magazines this is not the stimulus for increasing strength or size.

If enough time is not left between sets lactic acid will accumulate not only in the muscle but in the blood as well. Once in the blood, the lactic acid is transported to all parts of the body. When lactic acid is transported to other muscles it negatively affects their performance as well. In other words, training one muscle group to failure is going to decrease the quantity and quality of work done by another muscle group.

A build-up of lactic acid can increase the chance of injury. When muscle fibers start to drop out of an exercise technique starts to get sloppy. Muscle fiber dropout also makes it more difficult for motor patterns to be established, i.e., people who are doing a new exercise will have greater difficulty learning the exercise if they are building up lactic acid.

You should rest at least 2 minutes, and preferably 3 minutes between sets. This will allow you to maximize the intensity that you can use and the results that you get. Training with long rest periods increases the amount of time required to do a training session. This is often a concern for busy people who only have a short time in which to train. The 3-5 minute rest period between sets can be accomplished by having the athlete train using supersets (two exercises done in a row without rest between them) or circuit training. If supersets are done, the exercises should involve non-related parts of the body like biceps and calves or shoulders and hamstrings. Circuit training exercises should alternate upper and lower body exercises with only one exercise per body part. When the body parts are separated like this the alactic energy stores can be replenished in one part while the other is working.

3.4.3 Recovery

Recovery refers to the rest period between training sessions. The body follows a recovery pattern that starts immediately following the exercise session and can continue for as much as 7 days. Recovery can be divided into two parts: a fast recovery that occurs in the first 2 hours following exercise and a long recovery that occurs from 2 hours to 72 hours following exercise. The fast recovery involves returning blood lactic acid levels to normal, replenishing water stores, and starting the replenishment of the carbohydrates used during the training session. The slow recovery consists of complete replenishment of carbohydrates, this requires almost 24 hours, and repair of damaged muscle and connective tissue. The repair of connective tissue and muscle requires from 48 hours up to 7 days depending upon the extent of the damage. The best increases in strength occur when the muscles are allowed to fully recover between training sessions. If you follow the guidelines in Table 1 you should be able to work the same muscles every 72-96 hours.

3.5 Exercises

Split Squats

Purpose:
- Strengthen and improve flexibility in the hips to help prevent back problems.
- Help re-establish equal strength in right and left legs.

Starting position:
- Hold a dumbbell in each hand or place a barbell across the back of the shoulders.
- Feet are shoulder width apart.

Performance:
- Keeping the torso upright step forward with one leg.
- Allow the front leg to bend to 90°.
- Push off the front leg and return to the starting position.

Important Tips:
- Keep the torso upright at all times.
- Take a long step forward when you split.
- The back leg should be slightly bent.
- The back leg does not bend or straighten during the movement.

Squat

Purpose:

- To strengthen the musculature of the lower body.
- To improve strength for the leg drive.
- To improve core strength and posture.

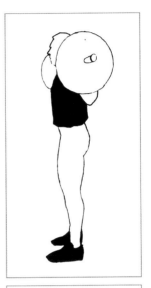

Starting Position:

- The bar is positioned across the shoulders with the load distributed across the traps.
- The hands are as close to the centre of the bar as possible.
- The head is up and the chest is out.
- The shoulders are back.
- The back is flat with a slight arch at the base.
- The feet are shoulder width apart.

Performance:

- Point the toes slightly outwards at an angle of 30° - 35°.
- Inhale deeply and contract the muscles of the torso to help stabilize the upper body.
- Squat down until you achieve the same compression you get in the boat.
- Drive with the legs and return to a standing position.

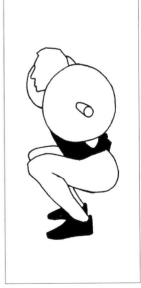

The Leg Curl

Purpose:

- Increase strength in the leg flexor muscles and hips.
- Maintain muscular balance across the knee joint.

Starting Position:

- Lie face down on the leg curl machine.
- Place the knees just off the end of the bench.
- Place heels under heel pads.
- Hold onto the bench or handles.

Performance:

- Keeping the upper body flat against the bench raise the heel pads towards the buttocks.
- When the full range of movement has been completed lower the weight to the starting position.

Important Tips:

- Try not to raise the buttocks excessively.
- Don't bounce or jerk the weight in the bottom position.

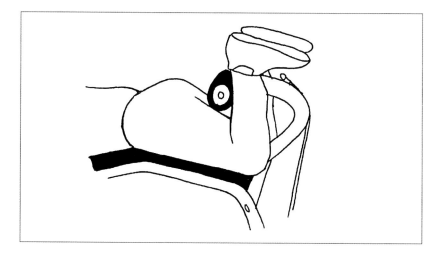

Front Squat

Purpose:

- Strengthen the musculature of the lower body.
- Improve strength for the leg drive.
- Improve core strength and posture.

Starting Position:

- The bar is positioned across the front of shoulders as close to the clavicle as possible.
- The head is up and the chest is out.
- The shoulders are back and the back is flat with a slight arch at the base.
- The feet are shoulder width apart.

Performance:

- Point the toes slightly outwards at an angle of 30°-35°.
- Inhale deeply and contract the muscles of the torso to help stabilize the upper body.
- Keeping the elbows pointed straight ahead squat down until the thighs are below parallel.
- Drive with the legs and return to the starting position.

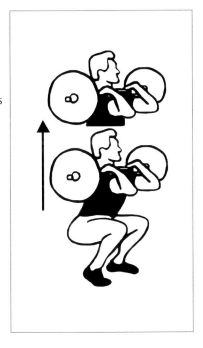

Hip Extensions

Purpose:

- To strengthen and improve flexibility in the hips to help prevent back problems.
- To help re-establish equal strength in right and left legs following sweep rowing.

Starting position:

- Attatch a cable or rubber tubing to the ankle.
- Kneel on a bench facing the machine.

Performance:

- Keeping the torso upright move the leg with the cable straight backwards as far as possible.

Important Tips:

- Keep the torso tight at all times.
- Don't rotate the leg or foot to increase range of motion.

The Deadlift

Purpose:

- Strengthen the musculature of the lower body.
- Improve strength for the leg drive.
- Improve core strength and posture.

Starting Position:

- Feet shoulder width apart.
- Bar close to the shins.
- Bend into a squat like position.
- Hips are low.
- Back is flat.

Performance:

- Keep the muscles of the back contracted throughout the movement.
- Initiate the movement with the legs.
- Keeping the bar close to the legs move the bar to knee height using the leg muscles.
- Once the bar passes the knee caps bring the hips through and stand straight up.

Important Tips:

- Keep the hips low during the lift this can help reduce the stress on the lower back.
- Keep the shoulders back and the chest out to prevent rounding of the lower back.

63

Back Extensions

Purpose:

- To strengthen the musculature of the back and hips.
- To improve core strength and posture.

Starting Position:

- Lie face down on a flat bench or on a back extension bench.
- The waist is just off the end of the bench and the feet are supported.
- Cross the arms across the chest.

Performance:

- Starting with the torso perpendicular to the floor raise the torso until it is parallel to the floor.

Important Tips:

- It is not necessary to raise the torso into a hyperextended position.

Trunk Rotation

Purpose:
- Strengthen the musculature of abdominals.
- Re-establish equal strength in right and left legs following sweep rowing.

Starting Position:
- Lie face up on an incline bench.
- Bend the knees to 90°.
- Arms are straight and extended towards the ceiling.
- Hold a weight in your hands.

Performance:
- Keeping the arms straight rotate from the waist towards one side.
- Using the abdominal muscles only pull the weight over and rotate to the other side.

Important Tips:
- Perform the exercise smoothly, avoid quick jerky movements.
- Don't let the arms collapse.
- Pull only with the abdominals not the arms.

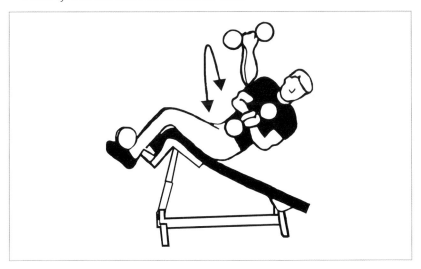

Seated Leg Raises

Purpose:

- Strengthen the musculature of the abdominal and hip flexor muscles.
- Improve core strength and posture.

Starting Position:

- Sit on the end of a bench.
- Knees slightly bent.
- Hands under the buttocks.

Performance:

- Contract the abdominals and raise the legs towards the chest.
- At the same time pull the trunk towards the knees.
- Slowly lower the legs to the starting position.

Important Tips:

- Keep the abdominals tightly contracted throughout the movement.

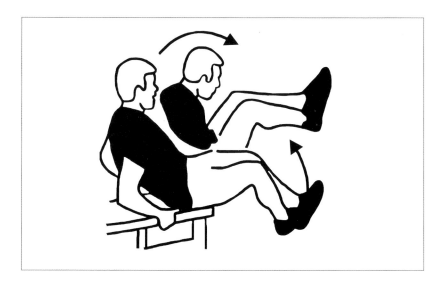

Lat Pulldown

Purpose:

- Strengthen the muscles used in the arm pull.

Starting position:

- Take a seated position.
- Take a wide palms down grip.
- Arms extended overhead.

Performance:

- Pull the bar down in front of the body until it touches the top of the sternum.
- The bar may be pulled in back of the head until it touches the base of the neck.

Important Tips:

- Don't jerk the body to help move the weight.
- Keep the upper body straight during the whole movement.

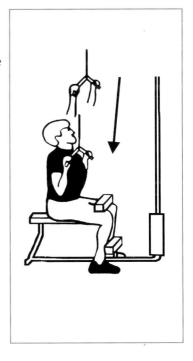

Pullovers

Purpose:

- Help prevent rib injuries.
- Improve trunk strength.

Starting Position:

- Lie flat on your back on a bench or across a Swiss ball.
- Feet on the floor.
- Grasp a barbell or dumbbell in both hands.

Performance:

- Begin with the weight over the chest.
- Lower the bar back over the head keeping the elbows bent.
- Lower the bar as far back as possible.
- Keep the elbows close to the head.
- Pull the bar back over to the starting position.

Important Tips:

- Keep the elbows bent to the same degree throughout the movement.

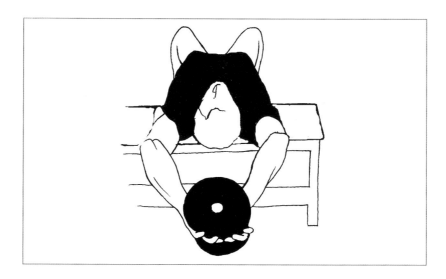

Seated Row

Purpose:
- Improve lower back and arm strength.
- Improve strength in the arm pull and layback.

Starting position:
- Take a seated position.
- Legs slightly bent.
- Back flat.
- Grasp the handle using an overhand grip.

Performance:
- Bend forward from the waist keeping the back straight.
- When the handle approaches the toes pull back to a straight body position.
- The arms start to pull as the hands reach the knees.

Important Tips:
- Don't jerk the body to help move the weight.
- Keep the back flat during the whole movement.

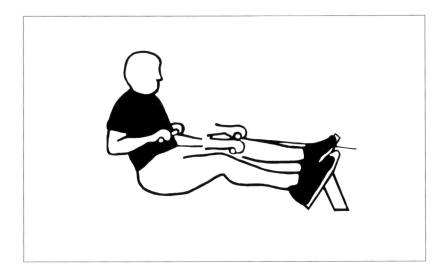

The Bench Press

Purpose:

- Help maintain balanced strength between pushing and pulling muscles in the upper body.

Starting Position:

- Lie flat on the bench.
- Feet flat on the floor.
- Buttocks, shoulders and head are in contact with the bench.
- The bar is grasped with a shoulder width or wider grip.
- The bar is removed from the rack to arms length.
- Inhale deeply to stabilize the upper body.
- The legs push against the floor to prevent slipping.

Performance:

- Slowly lower the bar to the chest.
- The bar should touch a point level with the nipples.
- The bar is rapidly accelerated off the chest.
- Press until the bar comes to arms length.

Important Tips:

- Don't bounce the weight off the chest, this can damage the sternum.
- Don't place the feet on the bench as this decreases stability.

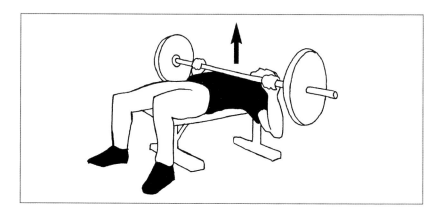

Bent Lateral Raises

Purpose:

- Increase strength in the muscles that stabilize the shoulder when pulling on the oar.

Starting Position:

- Hold a dumbell in each hand with palms facing each other.
- Sit on a bench.
- Bend at the waist so that the chest is on the thighs.
- Hold the weight just behind the calves.
- Keep the upper body straight.
- Elbows are bent slightly.

Performance:

- Keeping the elbows slightly bent raise the weight to the side.
- Raise the weight until the arms reach shoulder level and the arms are parallel to the floor.
- Pause at the top of the movement.

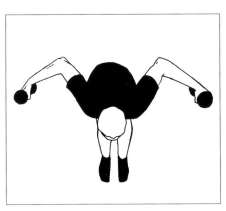

Important Tips:

- Don't allow the arms to rotate.
- Keep the upper body straight and still, don't sway or swing the upper body.
- Try to control the weight when lowering.

71

The Arm Curl

Purpose:
- Increase arm strength to aid in pulling.

Starting Position:
- Take an underhand grip.
- Hands shoulder width apart.
- Arms straight.
- Knees slightly bent.
- Torso upright.

Performance:
- Keep the torso upright without swaying.
- Bend the arms so that the weight finishes just under the chin.
- Lower the weight under control until the arms are straight.

Important Tips:
- Make sure the arms are straight at the end of the movement.
- Keep the elbows close to the sides throughout the movement.

Balance and Stability Exercises

Seated Balance

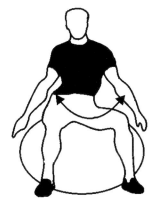

- Sit on top of the ball.
- Heel and hands are away from the ball.
- Rotate your hips from side to side and around in circles.
- Use your abs to keep balance.
- Try not to move your feet or fall off the ball.

Alternate Leg Balance

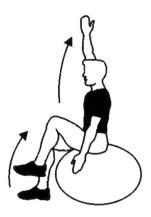

- Sit on top of the ball, hands at your sides on the ball.
- Slowly raise one leg and the opposite arm.
- Hold for 10 seconds and switch.
- To increase the difficulty rest the other hand in your lap instead of on the ball.

Single Leg Balance

- Sit on top of the ball.
- Holding onto the ball slowly straighten one leg.
- Keep the other foot still.
- Maintain balance using the trunk muscles.
- To increase the difficulty take your hands off the ball.
- The heel of the leg on the floor should not touch the ball.

Sculling Balance

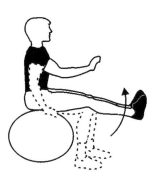

- Sit on top of the ball.
- Slowly raise both arms and feet.
- Once you can comfortably balance in this position try simulating the sculling motion with the arms and legs.
- Do not attempt this execise until you master the previous other seated balance exercises.

Single Leg Bridge

- Lie on the ball so that your shoulder blades and neck are supported.
- Hands and feet are on the floor, hips are raised so that a bridge is formed.
- Slowly straighten one leg. The other leg should be kept still and the hips stay high.
- Increase the difficulty by placing your arms across your chest.

Ball Bridge

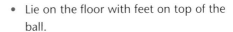

- Lie on the floor with feet on top of the ball.
- Arms are at your sides to help balance.
- Raise your hips until there is a straight line from your knees to chin.
- Increase the difficulty by folding your arms across your chest.

Wheelbarrow Balance

- Lie face down on the ball in a push up position. Hands on the floor, waist on the ball.
- Walk forwards on your hands until only your feet are on the ball then walk backwards.
- Keep your abs tightly contracted throughout the movement to support your low back.

One Arm Superman

- Lie face down on the ball in a push-up position. Thighs on the ball hands on the floor.
- Contract your abs to stabilize your trunk and slowly lift one arm off the floor.
- Hold the arm straight out for 10 seconds, put it down, and repeat with the other arm.

Chapter 4: Developing a Training Plan

The annual physical training plan is a map you use to guide yourself through the year. A good training plan has many characteristics that work together to bring you to peak form.

4.1 Characteristics of a Training Plan

4.1.1 Flexibility

The training plan is not the law. It is a guideline set out at the beginning of the year. It should be flexible because the exact response of an individual to a training session cannot be predicted months in advance. If the training plan is made for a crew, it should be flexible enough to take into account the individual needs and schedules of the athletes involved. A flexible training plan will have a greater level of compliance than one that doesn't take into account individual differences and unpredictable events.

However, there is a limit to the flexibility of a training plan. If the plan is too flexible it will give the impression of lack of organization. A poorly organized plan will not get you or your crew to your goals.

4.1.2 Goal Setting

Goal setting is the cornerstone of the training plan. Without goals the training plan and athlete have no specific direction. Designing a training plan without goals is like building a house without a blueprint – it isn't impossible but it is very difficult.

Benefits of Goal Setting

If you have a coach, both of you should participate in the goal setting process. There are several reasons for establishing goals for the upcoming season:

- Direction is established and priorities are set.
- Concrete goals increase motivation.
- Provide a basis for measurable success.
- Improves communication between athlete and coach.
- Helps develop psychological maturity for training and racing.

4.1.3 Establishing Goals for Rowers

Goals have to be realistic and attainable. There are two types of goals that must be set – short-term and long-term goals. Long-term goals represent the ultimate end point for the athlete that season. Short-term goals are then used as steps to help them get to the long-term goal. Short-term goals should be attainable in a reasonable period of time (several weeks).

A novice athlete can expect to make very rapid progress and should set goals appropriately. With good training and coaching it is reasonable for a novice to improve their performance by 30-40% in the first year. Experienced athletes up to age 60 can expect to see improvements of 2-5% per year. After age 60 there is a decrease in physiological capacity of about 2-3% per year. Maintenance of performance after age 60 actually means you have increased by 2-3%. This should be the goal for older rowers.

The amount of progress and the goals you set should take into account your commitment to rowing. For those interested in racing for fun at local races training 3-6 hours per week is sufficient. If you want to move up to larger more competitive races, you will need to increase the amount of training you do to 6-9 hours per week. In order to be competitive at major races like the World or National Championships or the Head of the Charles you will need to increase your commitment to the sport and train 10+ hours per week.

Planning and goal setting lead these athletes to back to back World Championships.

Do not be afraid to adjust the short-term goals as the year progresses. If a goal is not reached in the estimated time, it does not mean that you have failed, it only means that the time for reaching the goal was underestimated.

4.1.4 Periodic Checkups

Some method of monitoring the effectiveness of the training plan should be built into the plan. Periodic checkups help to ensure the set goals can be reached. They give you or your coach some concrete data upon which to base changes in the training plan. These checkups can take on a variety of forms. Monitoring of training log books, fitness assessments, or race results are all good tools. If you aren't seeing some form of improvement, take a closer look at your program to see where you can make some changes.

4.2 Periodized Planning

The training plan must be periodized. It is impossible to train all the necessary components of a sport at one time there should be periods during the year where certain things are emphasized while others are maintained. All elements of an athlete's preparation should be periodized including physical preparation, psychological preparation and skill development. Periodization is usually done by following the logical breakup of the competitive year into training phases.

4.2.1 Training Phases

The year can be broken up into logical training periods such as the preparatory phase, the competitive phase, and the transition phase.

The Preparatory Phase

The preparatory phase falls at the beginning of the training year. The preparatory phase can be further divided into general preparation and specific preparation periods. The general preparation is the first and longest of the preparation phases. Generally, 12 to 24 weeks are required for this phase. The goal of the general preparation phase is to improve on areas of weakness and to build a base for higher intensity specific preparation. Rehabilitation of injuries or muscle imbalances created during the previous season are corrected during the first part of this phase. During this phase general strength training, flexibility and aerobic conditioning are emphasized. A long, productive general preparation phase will allow the athlete to reach a high peak for a major competition.

In rowing, the training volumes tend to be slightly lower during the general preparatory phase. Almost all aerobic training will be done in category VI with possibly one each of categories V and IV. Because of the emphasis on category VI, cross-training can be used during the general preparation phase to alleviate boredom and help prevent overuse injuries. The specific preparation phase is 8 to 16 weeks long and takes advantage of the base developed during the general preparation phase. The newly acquired fitness is put to work in sport-specific situations. There is more emphasis placed upon specific aerobic, anaerobic and power work in this phase. Training volumes increase through the specific preparation phase. By the end of the phase, the training sessions should very closely imitate competitive situations as far as movement patterns, speed, and work/rest intervals are concerned. There should be maintenance training sessions for strength and general aerobic conditioning built into this phase.

The preparation phases are the ideal time to emphasize skill development. Since the work volumes are high but the intensity of the activities is very low you should not be experiencing high levels of fatigue that will negatively impact upon skill development or perfection. The general preparation phase is an excellent time to work on individual parts of a skill that may need perfecting (i.e. body position during the leg drive, feathering the blade, etc.). The specific preparation phase should see the beginnings of combining the parts of the skills into the whole skill.

Pre-Competitive Phase

The pre-competitive phase, or pre-season, normally lasts 4 to 8 weeks. There is a greater emphasis on the development of on-water speed during this phase. Categories IV, III, and II become more important. Often crew selection takes place during this time.

Competitive Phase

This is the phase where all the important competitions occur. In cases where the competitive season is very long it can be broken into early and late competitive phases. The early competitive phase becomes an extension of the pre-competitive phase in that there is a greater emphasis placed on physical preparation. The main competition for the year will normally fall at the end of the late competitive phase.

During this phase the emphasis is on technical work. The physical preparation is limited to maintenance work and pre-competition peaking cycles. All the training sessions should be sport-specific. Where possible there should be a combination of skill development and tactical development at the same time. This means that a certain level of ingenuity is necessary on the part of the coach and athlete in order to develop drills that will accomplish both objectives. This is the first phase that is placed into the training plan and the lengths of all the other phases are dependent upon this one. The development of physical preparation is usually of secondary importance during this phase. Training should be done to maintain the fitness level developed during the preparatory and pre-competitive phases.

Perfection of skill and development of competitive experience are the primary emphasis during this phase. Skill development should emphasize the perfection of the complete rowing stroke. The fine tuning of specific parts of the rower's technique are crucial during this phase.

Transition Phase

This phase follows the competitive phase. This is a period of several weeks, usually 4 to 6, where you take a break from training. You should keep active during this period by doing activities not related to rowing. This phase allows time for physical and mental recovery after a hard training and competitive schedule.

4.3 Training Cycles

The training phases represent the gross structures of a training plan. Each training phase should be broken down into smaller segments known as training cycles. It is through these training cycles that the volume and intensity of work are controlled. The goal of training cycles is to control fatigue so that progress can continue for a longer period of time without overtraining. This is accomplished by alternating period of hard work with periods of easy work or recovery. It is during the recovery or reduced training periods where your body adapts to the hard work and gets better. If a training program is not broken into cycles it is much less effective and quickly leads to staleness.

There are two types of training cycles that we will discuss, the macrocycle and the microcycle. Macrocycles can vary in length from 2 to 6 weeks but are typically about 4 weeks long. Microcycles are usually about a week long and represent possibly the most important training plan division.

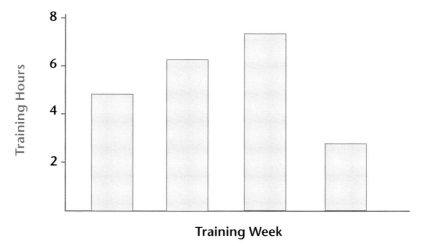

Training Week

Figure 1: A typical macrocycle where three weeks of increasing volume is followed by a recovery week.

4.3.1 Macrocycles

The length of a macrocycle can vary from 2 to 6 weeks in duration. The length of a macrocycle can be determined in several ways:

• The time it takes to learn a part of a skill.
• The time it takes to develop a physical quality.
• The time it takes to master a tactical component.

All can be used as the criteria for setting the length of the macrocycle. The criteria that you decide to use will depend upon what qualities you need to develop (physical, technical, mental, etc.). Macrocyles for rowers should be relatively short, 4 weeks long, to provide adequate recovery and regeneration time.

Designing a Macrocycle

A macrocycle is made up of microcycles (training weeks). Each microcycle will have a general intensity trend, i.e. high, medium or low intensity, that dictates how a macrocycle looks.

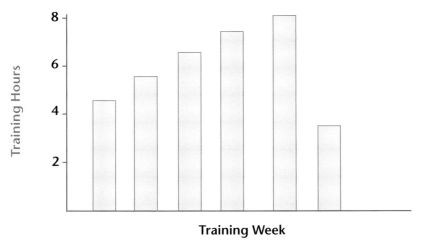

Figure 2: A macrocycle commonly used at the beginning of the year

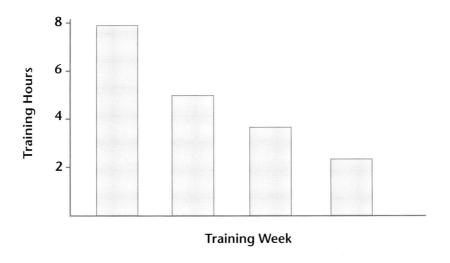

Figure 3: A cycle from the competitive phase leading into a competition

83

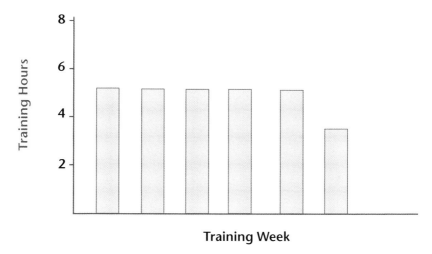

Training Week

Figure 4: A cycle that can be used by rowers training 6 hours per week or less

Figure 1 shows a macrocycle that consists of 3 weeks where the intensity of activity is increasing each week. In the 4th week, the intensity decreases and the athlete is allowed to recover from the loading of the previous 3 weeks. The recovery week in all macrocycles is very important because much of the training improvement will be seen following recovery rather than during training.

Figure 2 shows a loading pattern that is often used during the early stages of the preparation phase. The cycle is longer because the intensity of training is lower. The volume is maintained for a couple of weeks before an increase. This allows a rower coming off of a transition to adapt gradually to the new training year.

Figure 3 shows a macrocycle that is often seen during the final part of the competitive phase just prior to the major competition of the year. During this time you are tapering and there is a drop in training volume from week to week.

You must decide the type of macrocycle that will work best for your situation. Work and family commitments don't always make it possible to follow a traditional plan used by full - time rowers. It may be necessary to experiment with different types and combinations of macrocycles until one is found that works best. Experiment with different combinations of work and recovery weeks. Keeping careful records will help you determine which type of cycle works best for you. A test that simulates the race you are training for should be done at the end of the recovery week in each cycle. If you are not seeing improvements in test scores, you need to re-evaluate the length of the cycle you are using. There are some guidelines that you can follow when designing your own macrocycles.

- Progress from low intensity to high intensity.

- As intensity goes up volume comes down.

- Keep volume and intensity changes to less than 10% per week.

- Recovery weeks need to be included every 4 to 6 weeks.

As you can see, this means that you are not doing the same amount of training every week. You will have some weeks where you are doing a lot of training and other weeks where you have very little training. If you are a rower who is training less than 6 hours per week, you don't need to worry about varying the volume or intensity within a macrocycle.

You don't need the variation because your training volume is low. The purpose of training cycles is to control fatigue. You are getting adequate recovery between sessions, so a recovery week every 4-6 weeks is all you need to be concerned about.

4.3.2 Microcycles

Microcycles are the most important part of the training plan. If the microcycles are not designed properly it does not matter how well the rest of the year is planned. Microcycles represent the weekly and daily variations in the training program. The type of microcycle that you choose to use will depend mostly on the amount of time you have available to train and when you have that time.

One of the objectives of a microcycle is to distribute the training fatigue over the week to allow the athlete to accomplish as much work as possible while still having adequate recovery. There are four ways that this is commonly accomplished.

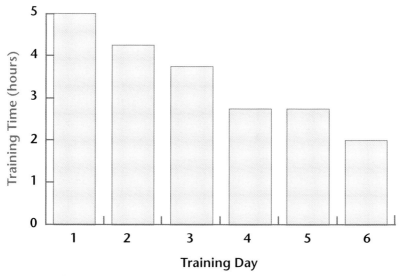

Figure 5: A front- or end-loaded week is ideal for a masters rower because the biggest training days can be on the weekend.

Front-loaded

In a front-loaded week, the first 3 to 4 days of the week have the highest training volumes. There is a continuous drop in volume through the week. This allows the athlete to complete the most work while their energy stores are full from a day off and lower training volumes later in the week. This type of cycle can be useful for athletes who go to school or work full-time. The training week can run from Friday to Friday leaving the weekend available for higher volumes of training. The seventh day of the week is off. This is typical of all microcycles, at least one day per week is set aside as a complete rest day. I would recommend you not participate in physically demanding recreational activities on the rest day. Failure to take a complete day of rest may make it more difficult to do the planned volume and intensity during the next week.

End-loaded

An end-loaded week is the opposite of a front-loaded week. The training volume is gradually increased throughout the week. Since the biggest training day is the last day of the week, you must pay closer attention to what you eat during the week. One advantage of this type of microcycle is you may be more inclined to push on the highest volume day, because of the time off the following day. This type of cycle is very popular with masters. It allows for a lot of recovery and short training sessions during the week and hard training on the weekend.

Alternate load

In an alternate load week high- and low-volume days are alternated. This method is used to ensure adequate recovery between training sessions. This type of microcycle is most effective with beginning and master level rowers whose recovery ability is less than that of elite performers. This type of microcycle may also be beneficial to lightweight rowers who are trying to make weight. Periods of food restriction will increase the time needed to recover between higher volume training days.

Even load distribution

Even load distribution is as the name applies. The weeks training volume is divided evenly over the 6 training days. Fatigue accumulates slowly throughout the week. The main disadvantage to this system is that athletes are tempted to pace themselves early in the week so that they can get through all the sessions. The end of the week is psychologically difficult if the intensity was too high earlier in the week.

Pyramidal loading

When using a pyramidal loading scheme the training volume peaks at mid-week. This type of loading is particularly useful during the first week of a macrocycle following a recovery week. It allows you to gradually get back into full training in the first 2 days of the week. Psychologically, it allows you to push yourself on each session knowing that the volume gradually decreases towards the end of the week.

4.4 Developing Your Own Plan

Putting your own plan together takes some time but it is very rewarding. It gives you a great sense of accomplishment and confidence in your training for the next year. You will need a calendar and a couple of sheets of paper. Follow the steps below:

4.4.1 Step 1: Set Competition Dates

Training plans always start from the major competition for the year and work backwards. You need to decide which races you want to enter and rank their importance. The final race of the year is normally the most important. You can enter up to five races a year before you start racing too often. Mark the race dates on the calendar.

87

4.4.2 Step 2: Set Taper Dates

The last 7-21 days before the major race will be set aside for a taper. This is covered in more detail in a later chapter. Mark these dates on the calendar.

4.4.3 Step 3: Set the Training Phases

Working backward from one week before your first race set the dates for the training phases. The pre-competitive phase will take you back 4-8 weeks and the preparation phase will take you back another 12-24 weeks. This will tell you when you are going to have to start back into your training.

4.4.4 Step 4: Plan Macrocycles

Plan the microcycles according to how they will fit your other commitments. Make sure to have a recovery every 4-6 weeks. The end of a training phase should coincide with the end of a macrocycle.

Now you have the general picture for your year. Microcycles don't need to be planned too far in advance. Microcycles should be planned at the start of the week.

4.4.5 Adjusting Your Program

Things happen that will ruin the best laid plans. Missing an occasional workout is nothing to worry about unless it becomes a habit. If you miss a workout continue on to the next workout as if nothing happened. Don't try to make up the workout as this can throw off your recovery and disturb the rest of the week´s training.

If something happens and you need to take a week off training, because of other commitments or injury, you will need to adjust the macrocycle you are in and the next cycle. Make the week you missed a recovery week and then create two short macrocycles out of the rest of the current cycle and the next one. For example, if in week 2 of a 4-week cycle you hurt your back and need to take the week off, week 2 becomes the recovery week. Now you have to adjust weeks 3 and 4 of the current cycle as well as the 4 weeks of the next cycle.

These adjustments can be made for up to 2 weeks of missed training. If you miss more than 2 consecutive weeks you will need to re-evaluate your year and start your training plan over. You will probably need to drop some of the earlier races to give yourself more time to train.

Chapter 5: Technique

When preparing to perform in rowing there are four major components of training that need to be included in an athlete's regime: physical, technical, tactical, and psychological. It is generally accepted that physical preparation is the main aspect of training required for fitness or performance and certainly is the most time demanding. Technical preparation follows physical preparation as a dominant training factor. Technique is dependent on physical preparation and relies on adequate strength levels to meet the demands of the stroke.

Technique can be defined as the method of performing the stroke. It is how you move the boat. Developing your ability to execute the cyclical rowing stroke in the most efficient manner increases your likelihood of achieving personal satisfaction and good competitive results while reducing the risk of back or rib injuries. The more mastery you have, the less energy is required to realize a specific goal. Good technique is directly related to high economy.

5.1 Technique vs. Style

Throughout technical discussions it is important to make a clear distinction between technique and style. Technique training is based on a model of the ideal rowing stroke and this frame of reference forms the rudiments of teaching the skills involved. Coaches and athletes collectively must have an understanding of a model that maximizes both biomechanical and physiological needs.

A technical model must also be flexible as developments in equipment or new scientific findings may influence current thought and practice. A model is malleable.

The elements of technique refer to learning the parts of the stroke. Correct practice of the stroke as a whole in combination with drills is how those elements are learned. The manner in which an individual performs the stroke can be termed one's style. Style incorporates distinct ways of executing the fundamentals of an accepted model of the rowing stroke. It may include traits of the athlete or coach's character and personality or be a specific way of performing a movement that is defined by the rower's anatomical or physiological nature.

Because you have your own individual requirements to meet the technical challenges posed by the rowing stroke, use caution when attempting to directly imitate the technique of champion rowers or scullers. A champion's style does not always represent a perfect model of the stroke. Their style is the result of how they have solved their own technical issues. Study their technique as an example of how he or she has developed their own highly proficient, personal style that successfully executes the elements of the rowing stroke. Use your observations to influence your own individual needs.

5.2 Methods to Improve Technical Training

Improving technical preparation may take place throughout the year: both on and off the water. The following suggestions are ways that you can better understand and learn technique:

- Improvement of physical preparation to develop the musculature involved in technical skills.
- Developing an ideal visual model of the stroke.
- Scheduling personalized instruction with a qualified coach on a regular basis.
- Attending a sculling/rowing camp.
- Including dedicated technical sessions on the water during each week's training.
- Performing technical drills to develop stroke components.
- Videotaping with review.
- Correct equipment selection for your body size and weight.
- Proper rigging of your boat and oars.
- Watching videotapes of international rowing events.
- Reading texts about rowing and sculling.
- Ongoing practice.

I	Proper handling of the sculls with minimal power application. Developing basic maneuvering of the boat.
II	Mastery of the sculling motion in a wide beam boat or team boat. Emphasis on learning the drive and use of body weight.
III	Transitioning to balancing a racing single with medium power application.
IV	Command over a racing single with technique maintained under various weather and water conditions.

Table 10: Steps to Learn Sculling Technique

5.3 Factors Affecting Technique

Physical preparation, how fit or strong you are, has a major influence on your technique. In order to execute the stroke correctly one needs to have adequate leg strength, core body strength and cardio-vascular conditioning. Poor physical conditioning will limit your ability to acquire new skills and decreases your chances to maintain proper technique under the stress of fatigue. Technical deterioration is often the result of a decline in physical fitness. For example, without core trunk stability and lower back strength it becomes very difficult for one to maintain posture through the drive often causing the body weight to collapse at the finish of the drive. In another case, without leg power a sculler cannot properly initiate the acceleration of the body weight that is an essential component of the stroke.

Lack of flexibility can also be a limiting factor in achieving good technique. The compressed lower body pose of the catch requires both hamstring and low back flexibility to meet the demands of the position. Either leg compression or upper body posture is compromised when flexibility is lacking. Poor hamstring elasticity will affect your ability to set your body preparation after the release while keeping your legs extended. Flexibility can be improved with practice and it is to every sculler's benefit to incorporate some stretching into daily training sessions. Finally, check that the boat you are rowing is in correct adjustment. Improper rigging is another factor than could affect your technique adversely.

5.4 When to Practice Technique

Following physical preparation as the primary training factor, technical training is next on the list of priorities. Devoting attention to technical training can reap greater benefits if done at the correct time of the year and at the proper time in a training session. Technical work should be done in a rested, unstressed state because of the concentration needed to develop confidence in the technique. Technique is best changed when you are not fatigued. Once changed you must learn to perform correctly at race speed. This is also learned best when not fatigued. Finally, you must be able to make the transition to maintain correct technique when under race stress. This preparation requires a great deal of time and is an ongoing part of training in the sport.

Within the annual cycle of training much of the improvement in technical training is done during the preparation phase, which emphasizes general and specific endurance. Next, during the following pre-competitive phase, technical changes need to be maintained. This period of training produces high levels of fatigue and technical training is not optimum at this time. The later competitive phase, which includes sharpening and peaking, again calls for a return to technical training to perfect skill and apply it to racing situations.

On a daily level, technical work should be done at the beginning of the training session and may be included as part of the warm-up. Again, technical changes are best produced in a rested, concentrated state. Perform the elements or drills that you acquired in the previous training session, continue to perfect the skills that you are working on, and gradually apply those skills in identical conditions to competition. Designating an entire session to technique is a necessary part of the weekly training cycle and should be limited to a maximum of one hour. Because of the high degree of concentration required it is easy to become quite fatigued by the end of such a session. Rest days should be scheduled separately.

5.5 Causes of Technical Error

Technical improvement can often be delayed because of incorrect learning. The quicker an error can be corrected the faster the rate of progress. Mistakes have causes and identifying the grounds for the fault help direct the corrective route to take. An athlete may be responsible for faulty technique due to psychological limitation (satisfaction with a low level of skill), poor physical preparation (strength, coordination), misunderstanding of the correct movement pattern, fatigue, incorrect grasp of the handles, or morale (lack of confidence or fear). The approach of a coach can also cause technical problems due to an inadequate or incorrect teaching style, an inability to individualize teaching based on an athlete's needs, or a coaching style that is characterized by lack of patience. On the non-human level, the use of poor quality equipment, adverse weather conditions (cold, wind, waves), and an unorganized training program can contribute heavily to your technical troubles and insufficiencies.

5.6 Principles of Sculling Technique

Basic Concepts

To move the boat through the water is the goal of each stroke we take. Whether sculling for recreation or training intensively for competition there are concepts that need to be applied to all styles. Rowing is founded on these axioms, which then help to form a model of the stroke. Details of how these technical points are executed may vary with personal sculling or coaching style. The purpose of the following section is to give a holistic picture of the technique, an overview that can be used as a platform for better understanding the dynamics of the stroke.

The stroke is built on basics and these fundamentals will hold true overtime. How well you are able to understand and perform the skills will grow with correct practice.

The stroke cycle is fundamentally divided into four main parts: The catch is when the blade enters the water; the drive is when the blades are in the water for the forward propulsion; the finish or release is the completion of the drive when the blades are taken out of the water; the recovery is the part of the stroke when the blades are over the water preparing to take the next catch.

The acceleration phase of the stroke is from the catch through the drive until the blade is released from the water and the arms/body swing following through. The deceleration phase of the stroke takes place during the remaining part of the recovery until the catch is taken. Correct timing and application of power contributes to the boat maintaining a given speed. The stroke cycle is fluent and rhythmical without any interruption of the movement.

Boat Movement

A boat should "run" smoothly in the water without noticeable "checking" or dunking, without irregularities in propulsion, and should not be adversely affected by changes in stroke rate or under difficult weather conditions. The hull needs to keep as level and as stable a position as possible while holding on course. Any vertical or radical movements will disrupt the run of the boat.

Blade Work

Stability of the hull is evident by one's ability to keep the blades off the water during the recovery without touching the water. Contact with the water causes friction and retards the movement of the boat. During the drive the water reacts with the blade of the oar to do it's job in moving the boat forward. The blade is our tool for the application of work and is designed to naturally set its own depth in the water. Anchoring the blade in the water and moving past the point where the water holds the blade is the only indicator we have of the work being done. Executing clean effective catches and releases are paramount to the uninterrupted flow of the boat.

Hand Placement

The oar is the instrument we use to transmit our body weight to the boat. In order to use the oar properly, it must be held correctly. This is a technical priority. Improper hand placement will block the ability to use the body weight effectively and will unnecessarily complicate the feather and squaring motion of the blades.

The way the hands are placed on the handles does not represent a gripping action. In sculling, the handles are small and will rest in the fingertips with the surface of the palm off the handle. Establish your hold with the blades square (vertical) in the water; this is the position the blade will be in during power application and is the reference point for placing the hands on the handle. Sitting at half slide with arms extended, square the blades letting them float in the water at their natural level, and then position your hands so the tips of your fingers curve over the handle in a hook grasp and your thumb is on the end of the handle. The base of the fingers, back of the hand, and wrist should be straight. As the hands draw towards the body the elbow/forearm complex moves laterally following the arc of the handles to keep the hand/wrist/forearm level with the oar handle. The thumb places subtle lateral pressure into the oarlock. Acceleration of the body weight during the drive creates the momentum to release and feather the blade with a minimum of effort. Feathering and squaring is the result of small actions at the blade and handle that allow gravity to set the sleeve of the oar in the oarlock. The hands need not work to "turn" the handles but need to develop a lightness of touch that lets the natural impetus within the stroke initiate the movements. This cannot happen unless the hand placement is correct to begin with.

Use of Body Weight

Rowing uses the body weight to move the boat. Rowing is not defined as a "pulling" action; a levering action to propel the boat forward would be more accurate. By learning how to use your body weight you will learn how to effectively move the boat. Body weight must be transferred to the foot stretcher as quickly as possible, when the catch is taken, without disturbing the run of the boat. Leg power is the initiating force to employ the body weight. By keeping the feet firmly in contact with the foot stretcher and pressure of the oar's collar against the oarlock the body weight can be accelerated through the drive to increase the speed of the boat. All applied power needs to be utilized for the forward propulsion of the boat without hindering its movement and the resulting energy from the drive will initiate the release with smooth flow into the recovery.

The length of one's stroke will be determined by the well-timed use of one's weight and posture. Moving a boat well involves tempo, correct timing entering the water and correct timing exiting the water. The finish of the stroke is determined by the inability to further maintain the body weight on the oars. With no further use of weight, effective work is not being done and there is no sense to keep the blades in the water longer than necessary. The catch is the signal to simultaneously begin the drive with entry of the blade in the water. The length of one's stroke can increase with practice, improved balance or flexibility but should not try to be accomplished through random pulling at the finish, over-reaching at catch, or through the collapse of posture.

Posture

Sound upright posture or to use the Fairbairnism, "freely erect" posture, is important for the proper application of body weight. Vertical orientation of posture allows the core trunk muscles to support the body weight during finish of the stroke allowing the oar handles to rebound lively through the release. Keeping the head up with the chin held level, eyes focused above the horizon, and the rib cage lifted provide the stability the body needs to "hang" its weight on the oar handles. Posture is of particular importance at the catch and release, transition points of the stroke, when the weight changes direction. Collapsing of posture at either of these points drives the boat down into the water and this vertical motion of the hull creates wakes slowing the boat, disrupting the run.

Posture can be practiced out of the boat throughout the day to be transferred into the boat during training sessions. Stand and sit tall; correcting slumping or forward-head posture while working on your computer or driving your car will improve your posture in the boat.

Specific strengthening exercises can also be done using weights, calisthenics, or a therapy ball to develop weak postural muscles.

Rhythm

Taking good strokes relies on maintaining rhythm between the acceleration and deceleration phases of the stroke to keep the boat moving at a constant speed. Ratio between the time on the drive and time spent on the recovery is usually 1:2 or 1:3; only at very high race cadences will the ratio be closer to 1:1. The rhythm of the stroke is fluent and uninterrupted.

It links an explosive drive with a relaxation phase on the recovery after the hands and body are set. Relaxation is active and posture needs to be comfortably maintained as the boat runs out from under you.

The boat approaches its slowest speed as you near the catch and its fastest speed after the moment of release. So, again, at these transition areas care needs to be taken to maintain posture and rhythm to keep the hull steady.

Rhythm is greatly aided by good breathing habits. To breathe fully the posture of the upper body needs to be straight so the diaphragm can act freely. As in weightlifting, work is performed with the breath held under pressure.

Exhale at the release then breathe in during the recovery just before and during the catch. When racing your breathing rate is elevated and often a second exhalation is needed on the recovery to expel additional CO_2.

Training at different paces and intensities will help accustom you to comfortable breathing patterns.

Balance

Symmetry of movements, proper use of body weight, and good blade work positively affect the balance of the boat. Balance is the result of all the elements of the stroke working together; allowing you to keep the blades above the water during the recovery and then use the boat as a "platform" for levering your weight.

Accelerating the body weight through a smooth transition at the release with level hands will assist the stability of the boat. Fluency will maintain balance just as abrupt, rough motions will disturb it. The balance of the boat is of decisive importance in competitive rowing especially under poor water conditions. Although an individual sense of equilibrium varies, it can be trained to learn correct righting reactions through drills such as: an exaggerated slow slide forward, pause drills, or balancing the boat after several hard strokes.

5.7 Main Elements of Technique

Finish just before release:

Head is up with focus of the eyes above the horizon. Rib cage is lifted to keep posture.

Release - flat wrists:

The release is timed with completion of the leg drive. Hands/wrists/forearms remain level with the oar handle to keep the body weight on the blade. Handles must stay up to keep the blades buried. Hands remain in front of the torso.

Hands/body away:

Fluency of the oar handles at the release helps transition the body weight out of the bow and prepare the upper body for the catch. Head, eye focus, and posture remain up. The pivot point is at the hip to set the body position. Handle heights are established.

1/4 Slide:

Represents transition timing of the stroke from the release to the initiation of slide movement towards the catch. Head and body remain stable with the knees just breaking as the compression of the lower body begins.

1/2 Slide:

Correct blade height is maintained off the water while the slide movement remains steady. Upper body position is unchanged, except for the opening of the arms, as the legs compress.

Hand placement at the crossover:

The left hand is positioned slightly higher and to the stern of the right hand at the crossover. The right hand nests behind the left hand. The wrists are flat.

3/4 Slide:

Preparation begins for the change of direction at the catch. Upper body posture remains unchanged as the arms open following the oar handles. The legs continue to compress.

Blade height off water:

Blade height should be sufficient to allow the squaring of the blade without a change in the level of the shaft.

Full slide/catch position:

Opening of the hands laterally outside the gunnels of the boat, with blades square, the catch is taken at the final moment of compression. It is the last motion of the recovery.

Blade depth at catch:

Only the blade needs to be buried. Avoid too much shaft in the water.

Hand placement on the handle-catch:

The oar handles rest in the hook of the fingers.

1/4 Drive:

The application of weight on the foot stretchers and oar handles is initiated by the leg drive. Head and posture remains erect to link the lower body and upper body weight.

1/2 Drive:

The body weight continues to accelerate as the upper body joins in to bring the oar handles through the point of the stroke where the oar shaft is perpendicular to the boat.

3/4 Drive:

The leg drive motion maintains emphasis, continuing to accelerate until the legs are fully extended. The body and arms continue their acceleration with the legs.

Finish just before release:

Posture and head position must not collapse as the leg drive and body swing complete. Handles remain high to keep the blades buried and to keep weight on the blades until the moment of release. Body weight remains over the seat without falling back towards the bow. Hands, body, and legs summate together.

Blade depth just before release:

Minimal shaft is buried reducing drag. Only the spoon of the blade needs to be covered.

5.8 Team Boat Considerations

Training and racing in double or quadruple sculls can help to improve your technique and provide interesting variety to your daily sessions on the water. Team boats are more stable boats than singles and give you opportunities to work on details that you may not have in the single. Many clubs organize quads to develop their competitive teams or to make efficient use of a coach's time. In addition to the social benefits, doubles and quads can be a more productive way to scull if your club is located on water that is not ideal for singles. For those who live in northern climates, early spring rowing is safer in team boats than in singles due to cold-water temperatures and higher risks of capsizing.

Team boat rowing requires working together as a crew to move the boat. This necessitates a willingness to blend your sculling styles together to build one style for the boat. Uniform power application and timing in all seats has to be developed for the boat to be responsive. Team boats travel faster in the water than singles do, so both catch and releases have to sharpen and your reaction time needs to quicken.

These skills are beneficial if transferred to your single sculling technique too. If you plan to compete seriously in a team boat, it is advantageous to spend a high percentage of your time training in that boat. Because of the different hull speeds, time in the boat is needed to groove modified motor patterns and nervous system reactivity.

Finding a good double-scull partner is not always an easy task. You need someone who shares the same commitment and goals that you have. A partner need not be the same as you in terms of single speed, personality, or style but does need to be willing to work together for the sake of the boat. You can learn a lot from sculling with better scullers than yourself. In a quadruple scull there should not be severe discrepancy between the stronger and weaker scullers. Working with a coach is very desirable with team boats to balance personalities and assist in making decisions for the boat. Every seat in the boat needs to have a role. In a double, the better technician can sit in the bow and be responsible for commands and steering.

The stronger sculler can stroke. In a quad, the stroke-seat sets the rhythm, the three-seat links the bow pair to the stroke; the two-seat calls commands, and the bow-seat steers. On a buoyed racecourse, the stroke seat has a better vantage point to steer during the race. In practice, you should try different seating combinations.

5.9 Switching Between Sculling and Sweep

If you have the option, learn to scull before you row in a sweep boat. The rationale for this is simple. Sculling is a symmetrical motion that incorporates equal learning on both sides of the body. The movements of the hands are finer and the balance of the single more delicate than any other hull size. By sculling you acquire watermanship, finesse and a repertoire of skills that can later be applied to team boat sculling or sweep rowing in a relatively short time. If you can row a single effectively, transitioning into a sweep boat is much less complicated than the other way around. If you have only learned the gross motor movements of a sweep boat, your first outing in a single usually provides an interesting and tipsy experience. To transition into sweep rowing also has its challenges and to be part of high performance eight can be an exhilarating event. In the small boat class, rowing a pair can successfully rival the intricacies of a single.

Differences in body position exist between sculling and sweep rowing. Because you row with one oar, in sweep rowing the body rotates towards its rigger during the recovery while preparing for the catch. The core body weight stays over the keel and the outside shoulder is higher than the inside shoulder, following the orientation of the oar handle. The outside shoulder (opposite side of the boat from your rigger) maintains the lateral pressure into the pin. The outside arm is between the knees at the catch vs. sculling where both knees are between the arms. The basic principles of rowing agree with sculling in terms of the use of the body weight, acceleration, blade work, posture, and rhythm.

Each hand has a specific function when holding only one oar. The outside hand is responsible for extracting the blade at the release, placing the blade at the catch, and controlling the oar handle height. The inside hand (nearest the rigger) is used to feather and square the blade and assists in keeping pressure on the oar handle as it nears the finish of the stroke. Exercises rowing with the outside hand only or inside hand only help learn these hand functions. Placement of the outside hand is at the end of the handle for good leverage; the little finger should not fall off the handle and nearing the release the wrist/forearm complex rotates laterally to remain on the same plane with the handle as in sculling. Keep the oar in the hook of the fingers to avoid over-gripping. The inside hand initiates the turning of the handle, and then relaxes to let gravity complete the feather or square motion. The preparation of the blade for the catch (roll up) is a stylistic decision of the coach. Some coaches prefer an early gradual motion others a flip catch. Whatever the style, the entire crew needs to roll up together and catch simultaneously.

Sweep release:

Position at the release; head is level and posture supports the body weight on the handle.

Sweep catch:

Position at the catch; eyes focused ahead, posture maintained, and outside knee stable.

108

5.10 Indoor Rowing and Technical Training

Indoor rowing or ergging has become a major part of training for rowing in the last twenty years with the advent of the Concept 2 Indoor Rower®. For many rowers, this has made it possible to land train more sport specifically at home, while traveling, or in the event you can't get to the boathouse. The competitive world of indoor rowing has also extended the number of races rowers do and has opened a whole new side to the sport. Offering an objective way to measure training progress, if workouts or control tests are periodically repeated, makes this a useful tool. If you use the indoor rower or "erg" as part of your training regime here are some very important considerations to bear in mind.

Stroke Awareness

Rowing indoors requires the same technical attentiveness as rowing in the boat does. Rowing incorrectly on the machine will only create poor motor patterns that will become unattractive additions to your water strokes. The machine does not replicate balance or the exact handle movements of a sweep or sculling oar but requires the similar use of body sequencing and core muscular patterns as in the natural setting.

The machine is stationary on the floor and a boat is moving so how your weight acts is slightly different during the recovery. On the machine you move your mass, on the water the boat moves under you, as your mass generally remains stable. This is important to be aware of so you are careful with your body preparation and the posture you are rowing with indoors. When moving your mass forward it is easy to over-reach or dive at the catch because the machine does not need to be balanced; the boat does not tolerated this as well. A sliding frame for indoor rowing is now available and is gaining favorable reviews for feeling much more "boat like".

Hand Positions and Chain Level

When rowing, the chain connecting the handle to the flywheel moves through a guide on the front of the machine. This makes it easy for you to monitor the level of the chain on the drive and recovery. The chain should remain steady and level throughout the entire stroke cycle, there is no need or benefit to change the handle height when rowing indoors. Placing two pieces of tape, narrowing the size of the guide, can serve as a physical cue to keep the chain stable. The chain picks up tension with a minimum of slippage if the catch is taken correctly. If you notice a lot of chain movement before you feel the resistance of the flywheel, correct your posture and work on a better initiation of the legs. The hand placement on the handle is similar to that of a sculling grasp except that you are unable to put your thumbs on the end of the handle. Keep the handle in the hook of your fingers with the palm lifted off, thumbs gently wrapped under. The back of the hand, wrist, and forearm need to remain level with the handle. Allow the elbows to move laterally as the hands approach the body and keep the handle height at the level of your sternum.

Caution: Over-compression and Hyperextension

The ergometer seat travels on a long rail. Because there are no front stops, over-compression at the catch is easy to go unnoticed. Placing a piece of tape on the rail can subtly remind you of the limit you want your seat rollers to go. The absence of a solid seat deck can be contributing to hyperextension of your knees at the end of the drive. Usually paying attention to this is enough to remedy it.

Rigging Your Rower

The adjustments of your erg are as important as the rigging of your boat for optimum performance. You can adjust the resistance level with the damper setting, heel cup height, and the performance monitor position. *Drag factor* is the indicator of resistance created by the flywheel; its importance is equivalent to the adjustment of *load* in rigging a boat. There is a lot of discussion among rowers regarding which damper setting (between 1-10) is the best. The lower numbers represent *lighter loads*; higher numbers *heavier loads*. A general recommendation for steady state rowing is a drag factor of 100-115.

The lower drag factor prevents the wheel from excessive deceleration between strokes and prevents unnecessary loading of the lumbar spine. This corresponds to an approximate setting of 3 though it can vary slightly from machine to machine. Avoid doing short, low cadence power pieces with high drag factors. Drag factors over 130-140 place significant strain on the lumbar spine. It is not recommended to use damper settings above 5. Gravitate to the lightest setting that mimics the sensation of your boat speed.

Set your heel cups high enough so that you can compress comfortably but not so low that there is excessive sloping down of the legs. Try to get the same fit you have in your boat. The standard range of heel height in a boat is between 16-17 centimeters. Sliding your erg seat up to the foot stretchers and measuring from the top of the seat vertical to the bottom of the heel cups can measure your heel height on the indoor rower. The computer monitor is best set up at eye level or slightly above. Encourage yourself to keep your head steady and eyes focused forward. A low monitor screen will cause your head and eyes to drop negatively affecting your posture and application of power.

Feedback: Shadow Rowing, Mirrors, Videotape

Feedback while rowing indoors is as important as when rowing outdoors to continue to make adjustments to your stroke cycle. Here are a few suggestions for making those long hours on the erg more interesting. Shadow rowing is one manner of technical training to solidify your technique and build uniformity in team boats. Do not use the machine's handle but "row" using the same hand/arm motions that you would use in the sculling stroke to pattern new technical habits. You can develop better flow with your partner if you work one behind the other or side-by-side to match your movements. This can be a very valuable exercise during winter months when you cannot be in the boat together. Shadow rowing can be used if you have a hand injury that prevents you from holding the handle or for mental training when conserving physical energy is important such as during tapering for races.

Technical feedback while rowing on the erg can be provided by setting up a series of mirrors in front, to the side, and at a 45-degree angle to your machine so you can see yourself. Videotaping yourself during practice can be a great way to analyze your technique on the erg. The Royle Individual Assessment Tool can be used for indoor rowing as well.

Indoor Racing Season

Indoor races are on many master's winter calendars adding yet another competitive season to the annual cycle. Like any other races you enter, choose and plan your indoor competitions wisely.

Prioritizing a winter training event is a great way to stay motivated to train in the off-water season and keep an eye on your competitors. In addition, the Concept2® website (www.concept2.com) offers worldwide on-line ranking for a variety of age groups and distances ranging from sprints to marathons. If you race in the winter, be sure to periodize your training cycles to allow peaks and periods of rest that work within your annual plan. A coach or training consultant can help you design an effective training plan.

5.11 Videotaping – A Tool for Analysis

Over the course of the season it is important to have feedback about your technique and to have some way of monitoring your technical progress. The analysis of videotape is a good way to identify faults and to recognize improvements in your technique. It also gives you and your coach an opportunity to work together in assessing your level of skill. Videotaping is best done from a motorboat with one person driving and another filming. From the launch you can film the boat from the either side, each individual at the level of the rigger, as well as, from the stern or a 45-degree angle. Keep the motorboat at a speed equal to the speed of the shell when filming. It is also possible to film from land by having a boat row by or away from the camera. If it is possible, shooting from a bridge to get on overhead view is another very useful and revealing vantage point. To videotape yourself rowing on the erg, setting the camera up in various positions will allow you to see your stroke from different angles. Shoot three segments: from the front, side, and at 45-degree angle from the front. Use a chair or stool and position the camera so you can see the machine centered in the lens.

When reviewing videotape, the slow motion and frame-by-frame features on a VCR gives you a great deal of control for technical evaluation. Try to be systematic as you look at a videotape of yourself or another member of your crew. Use constructive criticism. The following form is an assessment tool that can guide your evaluation process and subsequent re-evaluations.

5.12 Selecting a Coach

Like finding good training partners, it is a gift to find a high-quality coach. Your personal rowing situation has a large impact on the type of coaching you can receive. If you are associated with an organized club, more possibilities exist to hire a club coach or take private lessons. Rowing in an isolated situation such as from your home or at a weekend cabin makes your commitment to improvement and willingness to travel more of a factor in finding a coach to work with. Researching local clubs may be very worthwhile if the club has a coach who gives private lessons. Another alternate is to attend a sculling camp for a week or weekend to get intensive coaching, advice, and videotape analysis. The sculling camp atmosphere is usually very motivating and allows you to meet other members of the rowing community from around the world. Cost is certainly a consideration in working with a coach. With some clubs coaching is included in your membership, with others you pay a fee per private lesson. Logistics aside, you want to have a coach that is knowledgeable of the sport and is able to develop a rapport with you so that you can improve. You need not always be compatible in terms of personality, but you do have to respect the coach's ability to sense where you need to be developed: physically or psychologically. The relationship between experienced rowers and coaches is often a working relationship with more dialogue and communication than might occur when coaching younger athletes. Ultimately, you have to set your own priorities in terms of lesson time, travel distance, cost, and the coaches available in your area to determine which coach is the best for you.

5.13 Royle Individual Technical Assessment

The R.I.T.A. is tool for evaluating rowing or sculling technique. It is best used in conjunction with videotape analysis. As a means of self-analysis, athletes may rate their own performance factors. An athlete and coach, however, should perform this exercise together, each rating the performance factors, comparing scores, and then working together to identify the factors that will improve the athlete's technical score over a determined period of time.

Grade each factor from 1-10:

1= Poor-, 2= Poor, 3= Poor+, 4= Fair–, 5= Fair, 6= Fair+, 7= Good-, 8= Good, 9= Good+, 10= Excellent.

Technical Factor	Comments	Grade
CATCH		
Head alignment		
Focus of eyes		
Level of chin		
Position of shoulders		
Posture of trunk & chest		
Lower body compression		
Leg alignment		
Hand placement on handle		
Quickness of blade placement		
Blade depth at placement		
	Section Point Total:	
DRIVE		
Initiation of leg drive		
Position of shoulders		
Blade depth		
Hand level		
Use of bodyweight		
Quality of acceleration		
Maintenance of posture		
Head alignment		
Maintenance of eye focus		
Relaxed facial expression		
	Section Point Total:	
FINISH		
Head alignment		
Focus of eyes		
Position of shoulders		
Posture of trunk & chest		
Position of handles at release		
Relative to body		
Clean release from water		
Level of hand/wrist/forearm complex at release		
Timing between completion of leg drive & release		
Handle height		
Maintenance of acceleration		
	Section Point Total:	

Technical Factor	Comments	Grade
RECOVERY		
Accelerated movement of hands away from release		
Timing of weight transfer onto the stretcher		
Hand/wrist position		
Body preparation during 1st half of recovery		
Posture		
Blade height off water		
Balance		
Body position during 2nd half of recovery while compressing		
Full feather/squaring of blade		
Shoulder/arm position before catch (sculling) or trunk rotation (sweep)		
	Section Point Total:	
BOAT QUALITIES		
Hull at the catch		
Hull at the release		
Horizontal run of the boat		
Acceleration of hull		
Sense of liveliness		
	Section Point Total:	
SUMMARY		
Catch 100 pts.	*Your Total*	
Drive 100 pts.	*Your Total*	
Finish 100 pts.	*Your Total*	
Recovery 100 pts.	*Your Total*	
Boat Qualities 50 pts.	*Your Total*	
Overall total 450 pts.		

Comments:

Chapter 6: Technical Drills

Good technical skills are priceless: reducing risks of injuries, enhancing the aesthetic qualities of the sport, and developing efficient use of power. Drills allow you to concentrate more fully on a small component of a complex movement and better understand the stroke cycle.

The following drills outline different elements of the stroke and are divided into introductory drills for those new to sculling technique and performance drills for those who are refining their skills.

The introductory drills should be mastered before moving into other drills. When using performance drills select one or two relevant drills to be included at the beginning of your training session. Learn the movements and then improve your speed or pressure.

Vary your choice of drills to make your workouts more interesting. Be creative and enjoy developing your skills.

6.1 Introductory Drills

Alternate oar handle height

Sitting in the boat, the handles are lifted and lowered on alternate sides to learn the boat's reaction to the moving of the handles. The boat tips but remains upright.

Sitting balanced

Sitting in the boat in the arms/body away position, butt the ends of the oar handles together and hold in one hand. Try to rock the boat and observe the stability of the boat with the oar handles held in this position. The oar handles may also be held in this position when entering the shell to provide stability.

Lifting the blades

Sitting in the finish position, with the blade feathered, press the oar handles down into your lap as far as possible. Try to balance the boat. Note that the boat will rock but cannot tip over because the blades will support the position of the boat.

119

Rowing circles with one blade

Start from the finish position, blades flat on the water, boat balanced. Row with one oar only, leaving the other oar feathered on the water for stability. The stabilizing oar handle should be held against the body. Follow the blade with your eyes to see the effect of your actions through the water. Try placing the blade in the water, letting the handle go free to see the natural depth of the blade, and then placing your hand back on the handle to "follow" the movement of the oar. Row yourself in a full circle with one oar and then switch and row around in the other direction with the other oar. Use the least possible power and a loose grasp.

Building to full strokes

Once rowing with one oar has been mastered and balance reactions understood, progressing to the full stroke can begin. From the finish position, balanced, begin rowing with both sides starting with hands only and then adding in the motion of the body. Gradually make the stroke longer with the use of the legs and slide. Go slowly and do not apply any power at this stage.

Square blades/wide beam

Sculling in a wide beam, stable shell or a team boat supported by one rower holding the boat balanced, row with the blades staying in the square (vertical) position without feathering on the recovery.

Stopping

Learn how to stop rapidly. From a moving position, at the release, square the blades and press them into the water for a "braking" effect. Lean your body against the handles if needed.

Feathering

Turning the blade from square (vertical) to feathered (flat) needs to be accomplished with slight action from the fingers and the thumb avoiding excessive wrist motion. There are flat surfaces on the sleeve of the oar where it rests in the oarlock. Simple initiation of the turning of the blade is enough to let gravity complete the motion for you.

Practice the motion of turning the blade from square to feather with only one oar at first while sitting in a balanced position. Apply the ease of motion to the full stroke.

Backing

Backing is when you move the boat towards the stern. First begin by practicing gliding up and down the slide keeping the blades slightly tilted on the surface of the water. Then practice backing with one hand only, the other rests near your body. Start from the finish position, square one blade in the water, letting the blade float; push your hands away from your body.

At the end of the stroke, turn the blade feathered with the concave surface facing the water so the tip of the blade skims the water as you bring your hand back to your body. Try 10 strokes and then switch to the other hand. Then use both together. When you are comfortable with the backing motion you may add in slide length as you push away to make the stroke longer. Work up to backing for 50 strokes.

River Turns

Once you are able to back the boat down, you are ready to learn a river turn. You move your hands together but alternate the position of the blades. Using arms/body only, push your hands away from you with the port blade squared and the starboard blade feathered on the water; port backs, starboard is feathered on the water. Then take a stroke with the starboard blade as the port blade is feathered and skims the water; starboard rows, port is feathered. When you have mastered this you can lengthen your slide to take longer strokes. This is a quicker, more efficient way to turn the boat than simply rowing yourself around with one oar, especially if the water is fast or there is strong wind.

6.2 Performance Drills

6.2.1 Row Eyes Closed

In a safe environment row with your eyes closed for 10-15 strokes to focus on the sound and the feeling of the stroke. This is an effective way to appreciate the feeling of the boat and be attentive to the amount of noise your stroke makes. Try to minimize the amount of turbulence created while rowing especially at the transition points of the stroke: catch and release.

6.2.2 Open Fingers on the Handle

While rowing continuously, recover with the fingers and thumb open (extended), not gripping the oar handle. Relax the weight of the hands and forearms on the handles. Feel the weight of the oar handle in your hands. Control the handles with the fingers and rotate the blade just before taking the catch. Be conscious of letting the sleeve rest flat in the sill of the oarlock during the recovery.

6.2.3 Two-finger Rowing

The purpose of this drill is to learn to relax the hands allowing them to feel the natural path of the oar handles as dictated by the buoyancy of the blade in the water. Avoiding heavy gripping on the oar handle will allow the blade to seek it's own level in the water and provide perfect blade depth. This is a classic drill for learning a loose and relaxed hand placement on the oar handle. The ease of letting the blades sit at the correct depth in the water is obvious and pleasant. Relaxation of the hands cannot be stressed enough to develop sensitive sculling skills.

6.2.4 Row Easy

During the recovery normal hand placement is used. Once the blade is in the water at the catch, lift the middle, ring, and little fingers off the oar handle and draw through to the release using only the index finger and the thumb on the handle. Let the blades float in the water. There should be no tension in the hands, arms, or upper body during this drill. Relax and note how easy it is to keep the oars at the correct depth in the water. Perform continuously for 10-15 minutes when you include drills in your daily work out.

6.2.5 Pick Drill

One of the most common drills used by scullers as a regular part of the warm-up. The pick drill sequentially builds the stroke up to a full slide stroke. It is important that each position has a technical focus. Row 40 strokes at each stage. As part of a race warm-up 15 acceleration strokes can be included at the end of 40 strokes.

Stage 1: Arms/hands only

Keep handle height high enough to keep the blades buried. No body swing. Tall posture.

Stage 2: Arms/back only

Pivot forward from the hip: timing of transfer of weight onto the foot stretcher.

125

Stage 3: 1/4 slide.

Move just breaking the knees; timing the transition from the release to incorporating the slide.

Stage 4: 1/2 slide.

Increase the distance the seat moves to half slide; maintain correct handle height and posture.

Stage 5: 3/4 slide.

Prepare for the change of direction at the catch; head and body posture kept steady.

Stage 6: Full slide.

Complete the lower body compression; opening of the arms out for the catch. Full strokes.

127

6.2.6 Reverse Pick Drill

This drill is very effective for practicing the coordination of timing between the placement of the blade at the catch and the initiation of the drive. There should be a direct relationship between the commencement of the seat and handle movement. This drill emphasizes good connection between legs and back. Row 20 strokes at each station.

Stage 1: Legs only.

Row the first 1/4 slide of the drive keeping body position steady and arms extended.

Stage 2: Legs/body only.

Row full slide with the legs and body motions together keeping the arms straight.

Stage 3: Add arms.

Take full strokes with normal use of the arms.

6.2.7 Pause Drills

A pause of approximately 2 seconds interrupts the ordinary cycle of the stroke giving the opportunity to stop briefly and balance the boat with the blades off the water. It is also very useful for checking the position of the body at a designated point on the recovery. Pauses can be incorporated at arms/body away, 1/4, 1/2, or 3/4 slide. Arms/body away is an excellent way to focus on the acceleration phase of the stroke with a fluent release and complete body preparation. When the pause is broken the recovery can be continued by compressing the lower body and allowing the arms to open with the arc of the oar handles.

Begin by pausing once every stroke for 20 strokes, then once every other stroke for 20 strokes, etc...up to 5 strokes continuous rowing 1 stroke pause. Relax. Balance the boat with the blades off the water. Take your time and let the hull slow down. An advanced sculler can pause with the blades square. Double pause drills incorporate 2 pauses during 1 recovery.

6.2.8 Catch Drills

Correct placement of the catch is a difficult part of the rowing stroke. It requires precise timing, quickness, and relaxation combined. Catch drill teach you to place the blade in the water effectively without disturbing the boat. The catch is the last motion of the recovery; the blade entry must occur before the drive begins.

Begin from the finish position, the backstops, clear the blades from the water. Draw forward on the recovery – bringing the boat under you – and place the blades in the water as you compress at full slide. Do not initiate the leg drive. Take the blades out of the water and return to the finish position. Repeat 10-15 times with precision and blending the recovery and catch into one fluent motion.

6.2.9 Feet-out Rowing

The purpose of this drill is to practice correct release timing of the blade from the water while keeping the body weight consistently behind the oar handles. Feet-out rowing teaches to preserve the inertia of the drive in order to initiate an effortless flow into the recovery. While performing this drill, keep firm pressure through the thumbs on the end of the handles and feel the pressure of the water on the face of the blade. This lateral pressure into the oarlocks will assist you with a clean exit. Focus on achieving a sense of lightness at the release by learning correct timing. Pay close attention to "freely erect" posture. This cannot be over-emphasized. Spend 10-15' rowing feet-out 2-3x per week until you integrate the tempo.

- Remove feet from the boat shoes and place feet on top of the shoes.

- Enforce good upright posture throughout the stroke, paying special attention to sitting up tall over the seat at the release. Allow your body's core strength to support the finish turn with head up and shoulders still.

- Row continuously with firm pressure keeping the feet out. Maintain pressure with the collar into the oarlock.

- Time and coordinate the release precisely with the completion of the leg drive in order to keep the body weight behind the handles and transition smoothly into the recovery.

- Incorrect execution of the change in oar handle direction and follow through will allow the body weight to fall too far to the bow and the feet will come off the shoes.

6.2.10 Delayed Feather Drill

The purpose of this drill is to practice a clean and silent release of the blade from the water eliminating a tendency to feather under water. During a steady row alternate 20 strokes with the delayed feather/20 strokes continuous. Repeat 5 times for a total of 100 strokes. While performing this drill, keep firm pressure through the thumbs on the end of the handles. This lateral pressure into the oarlocks will assist you with a clean exit:

- Row at 50% pressure.

- Extract the blade from the water in the squared position.

- Emphasize a vertical release, enough to clear the lower edge of the blade before feathering.

- The square blade release must be accomplished quickly as the handles continue around the finish turn.

6.2.11 Square-blade Rowing

Square blade rowing is the top dog of drills. It demands and develops skill throughout several aspects of the stroke: balance, acceleration, blade work, blade depth, and relaxation of the hands. SBR involves continuous rowing with the blade vertical; no feathering motion is used. The emphasis is on clean entry and release of the blade from the water with uninterrupted movement of the oar handles. Balancing the hull should be focused in the lower body with even weight on the seat and no wobble of the knees during the recovery phase. For the SBR inexperienced, you may angle the blades slightly on the recovery so as not to catch the surface of the water with the lower edge of the blade. Strive for a perfectly square blade. Doubles and quads may rotate one sculler out while the others row with square blades. Alternate every 20 strokes. Good SBR will take your sculling to the next level.

- Sit at the catch position with the boat balanced and blades squared in the water.

- Establish your hand placement on the handles with the fingers in a hook grasp (as you would hold a suitcase handle) and with the palmar rise at the base of the finger gently weighted into the grip. The wrists are flat and the palm of the hand is off the handle.

- Begin the draw and emphasize a vertical release, enough to clear the lower edge of the blade. Be brisk without rushing and keep enough weight on the handles to keep the blade off the water. The hull needs to be kept stable using the lower body for balance.

- Stay loose, work with the boat, and follow through to the arms/body away position. Compress on the slide and place the blade in at the catch without delay.

- Maintain acceleration through the drive to assist the release and the balance.

- Begin by rowing 5 strokes with the feather, 5 strokes on the square. Progress to 20 with the feather, 20 strokes on the square.

- Gradually decrease the number of feathered strokes and build up to 15-20 minutes of continuous SBR.

- Variations for increased stability include: 1/4, 1/2, and 3/4 slide rowing on the square.

6.2.12 Feet-out/Square Blades Combo

This challenging drill is to row with square blades with your feet-out. Row for 10 minutes feet-out/square blades as part of your warm-up when you have flat water conditions.

6.2.13 Swinford Switch

Scull with the port blade squared and the starboard blade feathered for 10 strokes and then in 1 stroke, switch to the port blade feathered and the starboard blade squared for 10. This is an excellent drill for right-left coordination.

6.2.14 Half-blade Rowing

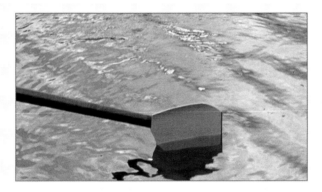

This drill emphasizes lightness of the blade in the water without allowing the blade to go too deep. Row 20 strokes with only half of the blade in the water. If you row with a hatchet-shaped blade, the shaft of the oar remains above the surface of the water. Feel for the lower edge of the blade to just break the surface of the water. Let your hands be light on the handles. This drill takes a bit of control because the blade is floating slightly higher out of the water than is usual.

6.2.15 Silent Pyramid

While maintaining elements of both relaxation and concentration, this drill develops rowing at full pressure. Completely relax the hands and upper body on the light strokes; maintain firm, powerful strokes during full pressure. Anchor the blade to lever the boat; avoid tearing the blades through the water. This is a terrific exercise to include in workouts for doubles and quads. Do at low ratings: 16-18.

- Perform silently without a teammate making calls.

- Row 1 stroke at full pressure/1 stroke on the paddle.

- Row 2 strokes at full pressure/2 strokes on the paddle.

- Continue up to 10 strokes at full pressure/10 strokes on the paddle.

- Reverse the pyramid back down to 1 stroke full/1 stroke on the paddle.

- Total hard strokes: 100

6.3 Overcoming Technical Difficulties

Fault identification and correction is a normal part of technical training. Critical concepts were reviewed to present a holistic model of the sculling stroke along with drills to target some of the main elements to be practiced. In this final section about technical training, some common mistakes are identified with suggestions on corrective measures. Ideally, through proper learning, try to prevent a fault from happening in the first place.

Tips on Correcting Faults

- Identify the faults to be corrected; isolate the components of the stroke to be remedied.

- Prioritize the primary fault to be corrected.

- Give immediate attention to correction of the fault; an athlete needs to understand the implications of the fault.

- Work on one fault at a time.

- Once the fault is eliminated, the replacement element needs to be demonstrated and learned. The athlete needs a model to learn from.

- Practice the fault correction early in the practice, right after the warm-up so fatigue doesn't interfere with the learning process and concentration is better.

- Avoid working on fault correction late in a practice session when fatigue is present.

6.3.1 Overreaching

Presentation:

In an attempt to get a longer stroke, the sculler tries to stretch too far to put the blade in at the catch. The seat stops moving but the hands keep reaching. This severely compromises the strength of the upper body posture at the catch and weakens the link to the leg drive. The idea of reach is an inaccurate attempt to gain stroke length. Stroke length is accomplished by correct lower body compression, use of weight, and timing. You cannot row longer than your body dictates.

Correction:

Once the body preparation is set by 1/4 slide on the recovery it does not change for the remainder of the recovery, keep the upper body position quiet and simply compress into the catch with the lower body only. Keep the eyes focused ahead and maintain posture. Practice the pick drill and catch drills.

6.3.2 Skying the Blade at the Catch

Presentation:

Just before the blade enters the water, the hands drop and the blades go high in the air causing water to be missed. This fault is deadly to your catch timing and dramatically slows the boat down. It is often a result of overreaching, collapsed posture, poor balance, or the eyes looking down into the boat.

Correction:

Practicing a correct recovery with a smooth transition between the last portion of the recovery and the initiation of the drive. This portion of the stroke is accomplished by the action of the lower body moving in and out of the catch. The levels of the head, eyes, and oar handles need to remain steady through the transition. Practice catch drills, pick drill, or square blade rowing.

6.3.3 Lifting Shoulders at the Catch

Presentation:

The sculler attempts to place the blade in the water by throwing the shoulders towards the bow vs. placing the blade with the hands and initiating the drive with the legs. This causes a great loss of power to the drive phase because the major muscles of the legs are not used. The sculler often thinks he "feels stronger" and is attempting to mimic a rowboat stroke not a sculling stroke by putting emphasis on an upper body stroke instead of a lower body generated stroke.

Correction:

It is paramount to keep the level of the shoulders even from 1/2 slide on the recovery through approximately 1/2 slide on the drive. The lower body is the focus at the top end of the slide at the catch; the upper body remains steady and quiet. The pick drill and the reverse pick drill are helpful.

6.3.4 Shooting the Slide

Presentation:

The legs are applied too early before the blade is placed in the water at the catch. The seat moves but the upper body and blades do not move therefore the forward motion is impaired.

Correction:

Improving timing between the catch and application of power. The seat and handle should initiate movement simultaneously. Shooting the slide can indicate lower back weakness or a heavy loaded rig as the body tries to take pressure off the lumbar spine. Improving back and lat strength can be indicated. Practice the reverse pick drill.

6.3.5 Breaking the Arms Early

Presentation:

At the beginning of the drive, the sculler immediately bends the arms to attempt to pull the stroke. This is a serious flaw that negates the use of the body weight and in effect prevents a proper stroke from happening. Breaking the arms early also causes disruption to balance and problems with blade depth.

Correction:

To use your body weight to row you need to develop a sense of hanging or relaxing your body weight between the points of the oar handle, foot stretcher, and pins. You need to allow the arms to be extended, yet connected, to be able to swing and accelerate your weight. Attempting to grab at the stroke produces an unattractive and choppy stroke.

6.3.6 Lack of Acceleration

Presentation:

Failure to accelerate right from the beginning of the drive is characterized by slow initiation of the legs. The boat will not pick up speed in a way that will assist the balance or a clean release. It can be the result of weak legs, an incorrect mental concept of the drive, or lack of an explosive quality to the muscle contractions.

Correction:

Execute a full and complete leg drive from the moment of initiation. Continue to emphasize the acceleration especially in the last 1/4 of the drive to preserve the momentum that has been built up. Leg strengthening or plyometric exercises may be needed to improve your ability to explode. Pausing with the arms/body away is an excellent drill to break the stroke into the acceleration and deceleration phases.

6.3.7 Breaking Wrists at the Release

Presentation:

As the oar handles approach the body, the wrists break attempting to release and feather the blade out of the water. This is usually accompanied by sagging posture, head droop, and the weight of the forearms and elbows drop below the oar handles. As a result, the body weight is not optimally maintained on the drive and the release can be clumsy.

Correction:

Proper acceleration of the weight needs to take place during the drive. If this happens, then there is enough momentum of the handles coming into the release to allow the water to assist the exit of the blade.

This is accomplished by keeping the oar handles in the fingers, letting the wrist/forearm/elbow complex stay level with the handle and moving laterally following the arc of the handles combined with quickness. The handles must be kept in front of the torso at all times. Handles pulling too far past the body make it difficult to keep weight on the blades. 1/2 slide and 1/4 slide rowing are good exercises for working on flat wrists.

6.3.8 Improper Hand Placement

Presentation:

The knuckles are white clutching the handle. The entire hand is gripped around the handle and there is excessive wrist motion to feather and square the blade. The arms in the stroke are consuming too much energy and the feeling of the blade is masked.

Correction:

Establish your hold with the blades square (vertical) in the water; this is the position the blade will be in during power application and is the reference point for placing the hands on the handle. Sitting at half slide with arms extended, square the blades letting them float in the water at their natural level, and then position your hands so the tips of your fingers curve over the handle in a hook grasp and your thumb is on the end of the handle. The base of the fingers, back of the hand, and wrist should be straight. As the hands draw towards the body the elbow/forearm complex moves laterally following the arc of the handles to keep the hand/wrist/forearm level with the oar handle. The thumb places subtle lateral pressure into the oarlock. Practice two-finger rowing.

6.3.9 Collapsed Posture

Presentation:

Chest and head are down at both the catch and the finish causing checking of the boat. The torso does not effectively support the body weight. Overreaching and skying often result from poor posture. At the finish of the stroke, the body weight sags on the seat cause the bow to sink in the water instead of riding level.

Correction:

Sit up tall with the rib cage lifted; chin level to the water, and eyes above the horizon. Throughout the stroke maintain this posture in a comfortable manner allowing your spine to support your torso. Do land exercises to strengthen the shoulder girdle (push ups, pull ups, bench pulls, bench presses), the abdominal muscles (various types of sit ups), and the lower back (prone extensions, back extensions). The use of a large therapy ball is excellent for doing stabilization and core strengthen exercises. Posture must be corrected in your daily activities as well.

6.3.10 Catching a Crab

Presentation:

The blade is feathered under the water and is unable to be extracted. Catching a crab could cause one to be capsized or catapulted out of the shell.

Correction:

Improve the timing of the release so the water assists in the clean exit of the blade. Practice the delayed feather drill and square blade rowing.

6.3.11 Excessive Head Motion

Presentation:

During the stroke there is excessive movement of the head up and down or side to side. This represents a loss of energy and disturbs the balance of the boat. It is often linked to weak posture, sagging body weight and poor body awareness.

Correction:

Correct posture with an emphasis on keeping the gaze of the eyes above the horizon throughout the entire stroke. Avoid looking down in the boat or dropping the chin at the finish of the stroke.

6.3.12 Late Body Preparation

Presentation:

At the completion of the leg drive, the hands sit in the bow too long before the recovery is initiated. The legs and slide begin to move before the body weight has been shifted out of the bow. The body is still upright with no pivot occurring at the hip. As the recovery progresses there is a lunge towards the catch to try to establish the body position at the last instance. Rhythm and balance are disrupted during the recovery. Poor flexibility can be a cause.

Correction:

Completing the acceleration phase of the stroke before beginning the slide motion on the recovery. Hold the knees down a shade longer to allow the hands to pass the knees before the slide begins to move; the body weight must be shifted out of the bow. Focus on continuous handle movement to lead the body away. Doing pause drills with the arms/body away illustrates the motion.

6.3.13 Rushing the Slide

Presentation:

Once the blade comes out of the water there is a rapid, uncontrolled movement on the slide to take the next stroke. The ratio is reversed and the oar is in the water longer than it is out of the water. There is no real rhythm or flow to the stroke.

Correction:

Re-establish the ratio between the time on the drive and time spent on the recovery to 1:2 or 1:3, only at very high race cadences will the ratio be closer to 1:1. The rhythm of the stroke is fluent and uninterrupted. It links an explosive drive with a relaxation phase on the recovery after the hands and body are set. Let the boat run out from under you smoothly. Rowing at low stroke rates of 16-18 or exaggerating the time on the slide are good ways to practice the discipline of slide control.

6.3.14 Incorrect Blade Depth

Presentation:

The blade is too deep in the water making the boat feel unsteady. Much of the shaft of the oar is covered by water during the drive. There are a few potential causes: the oar handle height does not travel level but lifts too high over the knees, the shoulders lift the blades in at the catch, or the hands raise too aggressively at the catch. Driving the blade deep causes the shaft to create turbulence and pull the hull down into the water.

Correction:

Relax the hands and check that hand placement is correct. Allow the blade to float at its natural level in the water without exerting energy to try to control it. The top edge of the blade will be even with the surface of the water. Two-finger rowing and half-blade rowing will teach correct blade depth.

6.3.15 Incorrect Blade Work

Presentation:

Incomplete squaring motion at the catch will cause the blade to knife into the water creating instability. Conversely, failure to keep weight on the blade until the release will cause the handles to drop and the blade can wash out at the end of the stroke.

Correction:

The feather and squaring motions need to be complete motions. On the sleeve of the oar there is a flat surface. This surface rests against the pin of the oarlock when the blade is square and on the bottom sill of the oarlock when the blade is feathered. With minimal initiation, the blade will fall from one position to the other with the use of gravity. During the recovery, allowing the sleeve to sit supported on the sill of the oarlock allows for full relaxation of the hands. Once the blade is squared, due to the force of the water on the face of the blade and the sleeve against the pin, little is needed to hold it in the square position, the handle can be kept loosely in the hook of the fingers.

Washing out can be corrected by maintaining handle height at the finish, correcting posture and practicing 1/4 and 1/2 slide rowing.

6.3.16 Short Strokes

Presentation:

Full compression and full use of the body weight is not utilized giving the stroke a choppy appearance. The breakdown of any major component of the stroke will affect the length of the stroke.

Correction:

Use all phases of the pick drill and reverse pick drill; complete hand motions, body preparation, and full use of the slide. Take care that blade depth is correct and release timing accurate.

Chapter 7: Rigging and Equipment

Your equipment and how it is adjusted is part of your technical preparation in sculling. Proper equipment set to fit your body size and physical capabilities make your sculling more efficient, enjoyable, and injury-free.

7.1 Boats

A large variety of boats are available on the international market today ranging from wide-beam open-water boats to narrow high-performance racing hulls. Boats are fabricated from wood and composite materials such as fiberglass, carbon fiber, Kevlar, or graphite. Performance factors, hull design, and construction materials usually determine the cost of a boat.

Choosing a boat that is best for you is an individual matter. Contacting boat builders, researching their websites, and having the opportunity to row different boats will give you valuable information to assist your decision. Purchasing a boat represents a significant investment and commitment to your sculling career. Prices for new boats typically range from $2500 to $7000 US. Used boats can be had for $1500 to $5000 US and are a good option for many first-time boat owners. Here are some considerations when deciding what type and make of boat to buy:

- What is your desired price range?
- What type of hull size do you need: heavyweight, midweight, lightweight, or flyweight. Ask the boat builder how body weight corresponds to hull size so you buy a boat that sits at the correct water line.
- What type of water will you row on: flat water, open water, fresh water or saltwater?
- What is your current level of skill? Do you need a wider, more stable hull versus a narrow hull?
- What are your goals: general fitness or high-performance?
- Do you want a new boat or a used boat?
- Do you want a boat with a high degree of adjustability or a boat that offers only basic rigging capabilities?
- Are boat builders close to your home making service and repairs easier to obtain?
- Do you prefer 3-point, 2-point, or wing riggers?

- Are you comfortable in the boat? Do you like it?
- Is the weight comfortable for you to carry and maneuver?
- Can you handle the boat alone?
- Where will you store the boat? Do you have length limitations?
- Consider the qualities of stiffness, weight, and durability relative to the cost of the boat.

7.2 Oars

Oar selection is another equipment decision that needs to be made. Prices range from $350 to $450 US for a pair of sculls depending on the builder. Traditional wood oars are made from laminated Sitka spruce and ash with a hollow shaft. Most synthetic oar shafts are spun from composite materials, carbon and graphite, around a mandrel and cured at high temperatures. Though composite oars dominate the market, there are still those who prefer the natural feel of wood blades.

Purchasing oars requires some thought regarding what is the most appropriate oar for your sculling needs. Factors include: price, materials, quality, stiffness, blade design, adjustability, handle size, and grip type.

7.2.1 Stiffness

Stiffness is the amount of flex in the oar shaft while under stress, during the drive. Stiff, medium, and soft flex shafts are determined by the construction of the shaft and the amount of longitudinal carbon included. Each manufacturer rates the flex of a shaft. Medium flex shafts are the most commonly used but depending on your strength and power a stiffer shaft can be ordered or a soft shaft if you want an oar with a slightly more feeling of whip at the release.

7.2.2 Blade Design

Blade designs range from the traditional spoon or Macon blade to a hatchet-shaped blade with a vortex edge and there are a few varieties in between. The symmetrical Macon blade is mounted on a longer shaft than a hatchet-shaped blade because the surface area is smaller. Overall length can range from 294 to 300 centimeters (cm). Rowing with this type of blade can be very good for novice scullers as it demands finesse and skill to row well with. Open water rowers may also find the Macon blade more advantageous in unsettled water conditions.

Hatchet-shaped blades vary regarding the curvature of the blade, whether the surface is smooth, and where the shaft joins with the blade. This blade type has a larger surface area than a Macon blade therefore the overall length of the oar is slightly shorter, typically 285- 291 cm. Hatchet-shaped blades are accepted to be more effective in producing higher boat speeds and most competitors use this shape. Each blade design, though, has both a different feel to it regarding handling in the water and "weight in the hands". It is to your benefit to row and test different oars before making your decision what to buy.

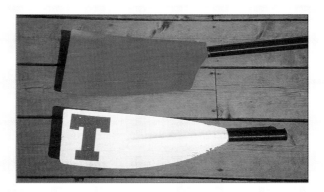

7.2.3 Adjustability

The adjustability of oars is a feature that has greatly improved in the last decade. In addition to the basic ability to move the collar, oars can be ordered with adjustable handles so the overall length of the oar can be changed within a 10-cm. range. This is a very useful trait if you row both singles and team boats needing to use different length oars for each boat or if you want to fine tune your single's rig, experimenting with different lengths. Fixed length oars can be ordered as well if you prefer a set length and do not require the extra choice in your sculling.

7.2.4 Handle Size and Grips

Handle sizes range from small, medium, to large. The diameter may vary from manufacturer to manufacturer. It is important to scull with an appropriate handle size to fit the curvature of your fingers. If you recall the discussion of hand placement, it is of the utmost concern to hold the handle in the hook of the fingers to properly connect your weight to the oar. If the handle is too large, too much energy needs to be exerted to hold the handle and it will be necessary to "palm" the handle with the whole hand to feel secure. If the handle is too small, there is a tendency to clutch as the fingers wrap around a handle that feels too thin. Diameter can be fine tuned with the type of grip used on the handle. There are many on the market from smooth to textured, thin to thick. Which sculling grip you choose depends on your tactile preferences and is largely a comfort issue.

7.3 Rigging

Rigging is the art and science of adjusting a boat and oars to meet your individual needs. The hardware of a boat such as: riggers, pins, oarlocks, foot stretchers, seat, and tracks can be set to optimize your biomechanical position in the boat in conjunction with your chosen oar dimensions and blade type. The make of your boat will dictate the amount of adjustability available to you. Generally, performance singles have the widest range of possibilities to customize your rig.

7.3.1 The Big Picture

When you rig your single you are setting the dimensions of the riggers and oars to maximize your biomechanical efficiency and comfort in the boat. Rigging is not an exact science as there is a good amount of art and "touch" mixed in, but there are some basic rules and references that need to be adhered to serving as a platform to fine tune your boat. Rigging needs can also develop over time. As certain elements of your technique get better, rigging details can be altered to support those improvements.

Keep in mind that you are working within a multi-dimensional framework when you rig your boat. You are balancing horizontal, vertical, angled, and diagonal measurements to create a leverage system that allows you to move the boat effectively. When you make one change to your rigging it affects the entire system and small alterations, at times, can produce large effects. Once you alter your rig you need to row with it several times to get accustomed to a new feel to decide whether the change was positive or not. Using a speed device such as a Speedcoach' that can measure meters per second, distance, and 500-meter split times, is useful for objectively observing whether a rigging change makes you go faster or not. Having a stretch of flat water without current is valuable for testing the effect of rigging over 500-meter or 1000-meter repeats.

Reference Points

The pin is the vertical axle the oarlock rotates around that extends upward from the end of the rigger. In rigging, the pin serves as a reference point for positioning yourself in the boat. The terms "through the pin" and "work through" refer to the centerline of the hip joint and the seat relative to the location of the pin. The hip joint axis may be behind, equal to, or astern of the pin at the catch position. Drawing an imaginary line from pin to pin provides a standard for the center of the hip joint axis to reach in full compression ready for the catch. In a performance single it is desirable to be at 0 cm, or equal, with the pin. In a faster moving boat you may work 1-2 cm through the pin. Your flexibility, skill level, and boat type can all affect your ability to get up through the pin, but the point here is to identify the pin as a reference. How you are situated in the boat helps to set the optimum angle of the oar at the catch and the release without causing the boat to be "pinched" putting the blade in an ineffective position which pushes water laterally against the hull versus propelling the boat forward.

Load is the term that defines the resultant energy relationship of the distance between the pins, inboard/outboard settings of the oars, blade size, and a sculler's physical dimensions. Load is cumulative within the leverage system and can be reflected in the size of arcs the blades carve in the water and the consequential stroke length. On a rowing ergometer, the concept of load is illustrated by setting the damper resistance high at "10" or low at "1" and is expressed as drag factor. Unfortunately, in the boat, there is no clear cut way for the average person to define drag factor and measure the load of their rigging system. There does exist, however, reasonable parameters to follow as we continue our discussion of rigging.

Keep in mind that more is not necessarily better when it comes to load. It can be too heavy producing undo stress on the lumbar spine, creating large arcs in the water, and making it a strain to increase your stroke rate adequately during a race. On the contrary, too light is a bit like trying to pedal a bike down a hill while spinning your large chain ring; you need to take too many strokes to maintain speed. Your individual body dimensions, strength, and race pace stroke rating, play a role in how much load you can optimally row with. Boat builder, Ted Van Dusen of Van Dusen Racing Boats, advised, "Rig for the end of your race," meaning set a load that is adequate to maintain race tempo yet light enough that you can increase the stroke rate for the final sprint when you are fatigued.

Getting Started

Before you begin you will need to get organized:

* Keep a logbook of all your rigging activities. Record the date and current measurements so you can retrace your steps if you need to.
* Have the correct tools ready: Hex keys, wrenches, a pitch meter, a long carpenter's level, and a tape measure with centimeters.
* Put your boat up on slings in a quiet place away from the distractions and curiosity of other scullers willing to give you lots of advice.
* Take your time and write everything down.
* Complete one step at a time.
* Once you measure, measure again.
* If you get tired, take a break. Keep your sense of humor.

Setting Up Your Boat

Before you start to take measurements or change the dimensions of your rigging you need to set your boat up in a way that will make it easy for you to work on it. Since a third hand is not always easy to come by here is a suggested way.

* Set your boat on slings of about the same size. To stabilize your boat, take a rod or stick (like a broomstick) and place it vertical next to one of the riggers. Using a large spring clamp – secure the rigger to the stick to prevent the boat from tipping.
* Level the boat end-to-end. Place the carpenter's level along a flat part of the boat such as the base of the gunnel; do not use the seat deck because there is a slight angle from bow to stern. If needed, fold and prop a towel between the boat and sling to level the boat.
* Level the boat side-to-side. Place the carpenter's level across the gunnels. When the bubble is centered, adjust the clamped rigger with the vertical stick to hold the boat level.
* Strap or tie your boat to the slings to further stabilize it.
* Bring your toolbox near by. Now you are ready to start.

7.3.2 The Steps of Rigging

Approaching rigging in an orderly, systematic way will make it easier for you to detect problems and make adjustments accordingly. If you are rigging your

147

boat for the first time, get all your measurements within a reasonable range. Once the boat is rigged, then make only one change at a time so you can assess the effect. Remember to write your measurements in a logbook.

Step 1: Spread

The spread is the distance between the two oarlock pins. This is a major measurement of your gearing system that will combine with your oar settings to determine the load of your rig. Measure from the center of the top of the pin to the center of the top of the other pin. To make it easier, you may have another person hold one end of the tape measure for you. Record the number of centimeters.

The range for setting the spread is usually 158-164 cm. An average starting point is 160 cm. If you are a smaller sculler a spread of 158 cm may be appropriate and if you are a larger sculler, 162 cm may be more comfortable. Moving the spread in creates a heavier load and larger arc through the water. Moving the spread out, lightens the load, creating smaller arcs in the water. You need to feel comfortable that you can open your hands along a horizontal plane well over the gunnels as the blade is prepared for the catch. This happens in conjunction with other factors but setting the spread is the first step.

It is of the utmost importance to make sure that the pins are set an equal distance from the centerline of the boat. Measure across the gunnels of the boat, take half the number of centimeters, and then measure from that point to the pin. For example, if gunnel to gunnel is 46 cm half of 46 is 23, locate the 23-cm mark on your tape measure, place it on the gunnel's edge nearest the pin you are measuring, and measure the remaining distance to the pin. It should read 57 cm if your overall spread is 160 cm (23 cm + 57 cm = 80 cm which is half the spread).

Another method to check if the pins are equidistant is to measure from the outside of the opposite track to the base of the pin and check that both sides are the same. You can use this method because the seat tracks should be set centered in the boat. Once you have finished setting the spread, measure it again. Do not change your spread casually once you have it set, you can use other adjustments to make smaller gearing changes.

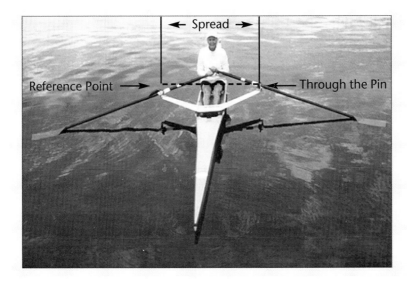

Step 2: Inboard

Setting the inboard on your oars is another rigging step that relates to overall load. The inboard is the measurement that is defined as the distance from the end of the handle to the blade-side face of the collar. Inboard setting is dependent on the overall spread and sets the amount of overlap of the oar handles at the crossover. Take half your spread and add 8 cm for a good initial setting of your inboard. Thus, if your spread was 160 cm; you inboard setting would be 88 cm. The inboard measurement serves as a way to fine-tune your load as you may move the collar in small increments to affect the load. Moving the collar towards the handle creates a shorter inboard lever and makes the load heavier. Conversely, moving the collar towards the blade, makes the inboard lever longer and lighter. Measurements from 87- 89 cm allow a great deal of adjustment. If you need a setting such as 86 cm, you also may need to select a shorter overall length of the oar to avoid an excessively heavy load.

Step 3: Oar Length

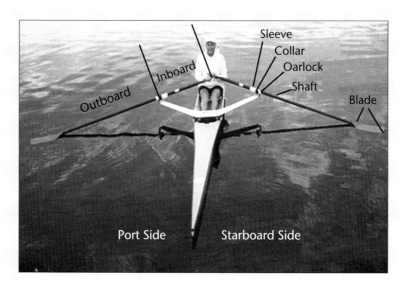

The third factor in determining load is the overall length of your oars. Your size, strength, and blade design will affect what length oar you choose to scull with. A shorter oar lightens the load; a longer oar increases the load due to the longer outboard. Outboard is the measurement from the blade-side face of the collar to the tip of the blade. A standard overall length for a Macon blade is 298 cm and 288 cm for a hatchet-shaped blade. A heavyweight man may increase these measurements by 1-2 cm and a lightweight woman sculler may decrease these measurements by 1-2 cm.

Some experimentation is needed in your sculling to set the overall length. Your needs may change as your personal style of sculling develops and you race at higher rates or gain strength. You also may find that you prefer a lighter load if you tend to be quicker and more reactive versus someone who prefers a heavier, power stroke. Remember that spread, inboard, oar length, and personal attributes must all work together. There is no sense to row with excessively heavy loads. Masters scullers and novices, especially, should lean towards lighter loads to protect overstressing the lumbar spine.

Step 4: Oarlock Height

When you sit in a boat, the first thing that you usually notice is where the handle height is. If you row club boats, you know that some boats feel "high" and others "low". This can be due both to the size of the boat relative to your weight and to the height set at the oarlock. If you row a hull that is too big for you, you do not sink the boat to the proper water line and you will generally feel too "high" in the boat; as if the oar handles come up to your chest. Rowing with the correct height is one reason to row the right hull size for your weight. Accurate oarlock height allows you to clear your blades from the water on the recovery and lets you apply your body weight properly during the drive.

Due to the crossover of the oars, in sculling there is a height differential between the starboard and port oarlocks of 1- 2 cm allowing the sculler to row left hand over right. This difference in the height setting gives room for the hands to nest together at the crossover and keep the boat level. The differential can be according to comfort as some scullers may like a little more room and some a less. The important point is that the boat stays on keel at the point of crossover.

Standard oarlock height runs between 13-18 cm and is partly a comfort or stylistic setting. At the finish, sitting with good posture, and blades buried, your thumbs on the handles should just brush your middle ribs at the level of your sternum. You do not want to feel that your handles are in your lap or up near your neck.

To measure height, use a long level placed across the gunnels. Set one end through the center of the oarlock and hang the other end over the seat. Use a tape measure to establish the distance from the bottom edge of the long level, to the bottom of the oarlock, and the top of the seat. Every time you measure height make sure to put your level in the same place and measure to the same point on the seat and oarlock to keep the references consistent.

Sliding the oarlock off the pin and changing the number of washers above and below the pin can usually suffice to change height in most boats. Note: When you purchase a boat ask the builder if the height differential is set in the rigger construction or needs to be set at the oarlock; if you row in a boat with a wing rigger check whether the starboard side of the wing is shimmed higher than the port. Some European clubs row right over left, in which case you need to reverse the height differential and raise the port side.

Step 5: Sternward Pitch

Sternward pitch is the angle of the blade away from perpendicular during the pull through of the stroke. A small amount of pitch, 4-6°, is enough to help the blade stay buried at the proper depth through the water. If a blade has too much pitch, more than 7°, the blade will wash out at the finish; too little pitch, less than 4°, causes the blade too dive deep. Sternward pitch is a fore-and-aft measurement usually taken at the oarlock but it must be kept in mind that it is the angle of the blade that we are concerned with, so knowing the pitch of the pins and the oars has to be taken into final consideration. The pitch of the blade = (the pitch of the pin) + (the pitch of the oarlock) + (the pitch built into the blade).

Measuring the pitch will begin with checking the pin. Ideally, if the pin is set at 0° it makes it easy to calculate your oarlock pitch. Unless you check it you don't know what the reference is. A commercially available pitch meter or a simple level can be used. With your boat set up level in slings, slide the oarlock off taking care to count the washers setting the height. Place a vertical level against the sternward face of the pin and see if it zeros out. If it does the pin is at 0°, if not, you may be able to shim your pin to get it to 0°, otherwise use your pitch meter to determine how many degrees you are +/- 0.

Adjust your pitch meter on a level portion of the gunnel. Put the pointer on 0 and then center the bubble on the level. Tighten the level so it is firmly in place. Place the squared surface of the pitch meter against the face of the pin and move the pointer until the level's bubble is centered. Record the number of degrees the pointer reads in that pin.

Next, put the round pitch inserts into your oarlock with the number of degrees you want and check that the top and bottom inserts are in the right orientation (read your owner's manual). Slide the oarlock back on the pin. For example: If your pin is at 0° and you want +5° put in the +5° shim. However, if your pin is +1° you need a +4° shim to give your oarlock +5°.

Once you have put the oarlock back on the pin and secured the top bolt, measure the pitch in the oarlock. Hold the oarlock at the mid-drive position (with the gate closed and star-nut pointing towards the stern) parallel to the midline of the boat. Zero your pitch meter and then place the squared surface of the pitch meter against the back plate of the oarlock. A spring clamp can be handy for this. Make sure the surfaces are flush to get an accurate reading.

Your measurement should agree with the sum of (the degrees in the pin) + (the degrees of the insert). If not, try again until you get the desired degrees. 5° is the most common setting, 6° may give you a little more bite at the catch and 4° a little less lift to the boat at the catch. Whatever amount of pitch you choose, make sure that both sides are the same.

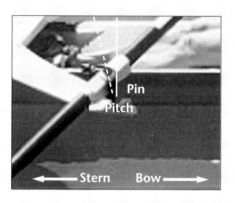

Step 6: Outward Pitch

Outward or lateral pitch is the tilt of the pin away from the centerline of the hull. The standard 0° to +2° assists the tracking of the blade in the water. You can measure it by placing your pitch meter on the lateral aspect of the pin and measuring. You can also see the effect of lateral pitch in the oarlock. With the pitch meter in place against the back plate of the oarlock, check your reading of degrees at mid-drive, swing the oarlock to the catch position and you should see the sternward pitch increase. Then swing the oarlock to the finish and you should see the degrees diminish to assist the release of the blade. Your readings should look like: catch +6°, mid-drive +5°, and finish +4°. If you have the inverse relationship, your pins could have negative lateral pitch and require creative shimming to rectify.

Step 7: Pitch in Oars

In North America, the majority of oars are built with 0° of pitch, meaning that the position of the blade is level with the flat wear plate surface on the sleeve. If you row with unknown or wooden oars you may have to measure your oars at the blade to determine if there is pitch built into the blades and take those degrees into consideration when setting the pitch at the oarlock. You can do this by setting your oar on a bench with a level block as wide as the blade supporting the blade and another support block under the handle. Place the blade face down on the block with 1" of the tip off the edge of the block if you are measuring a Macon blade or with the short side corner radius of the blade just off the edge of the block for hatchet-shaped blades. Then put your level across the wear plate surface to see whether it is at 0°. Shimming to get the level zeroed, .025" equals approximately 1° of pitch. If it is necessary to measure your oars, check with your manufacturer for specific instructions because there are variations depending on blade type.

Step 8: Foot Stretcher Adjustment

The foot stretcher adjustment should be placed so that you are able to get up through the pin at the catch and have about the width of a fist between the handles at the release comfortably in front of your body. You need to avoid feeling crowded by your oar handles at the release forcing unnecessary lay back and yet not have excessive room to allow the handles to swing past the plane of the body, thus losing the weight off the handles.

Step 9: Heel Height

Heel height is another measurement that can facilitate easier compression into the catch. The standard range is 16-18 cm from the top of the seat to the bottom of the heels. Many boats have adjustable footboards making this easy to change. If you boat has clogs, you may be able to re-drill and lower the heel cups to get a better setting.

Step 10: Rake of the Footboard

The angle of the footboard can be measured with a protractor or a goniometer (like those used in physical therapy clinics). Standard measurements should fall between 39°-42°. If you have poor ankle flexibility, it may be necessary to flatten the footboard to get into a more comfortable position at the catch. If you have good flexibility, 40°-42° is a desired setting to assist the leg drive in using the entire surface of the foot. Many performance boats have this adjustable feature, otherwise you will have to reposition the footboard and its attachments.

Step 11: Setting the Tracks

Once you have set your rigging dimensions and foot stretchers, you need to set the seat track so you do not touch either end and have freedom of seat movement. Most tracks are quite long giving lots of room for adjustability. Reaching inside the hull and loosening the small wing nuts that hold the track usually allow you to move the tracks. Do not take the wing nuts off; just loosen enough to slide the tracks fore-and-aft. Set the front stops to the stern of the pin far enough to allow you to get up through the pin in full compression but not so far as to hit the back of your calves in an uncomfortable way. If your boat does not have adjustable tracks you must do your best to get the best possible position within the dimensions available to you.

Step 12: Wing Rigger Adjustments

Boats with wing riggers offer some additional adjustability with regards to getting through the pin, setting height differential, and overall oarlock height if the amount available on the pin is not enough. Some care needs to be taken to position the wing in a way that maintains the trim of the boat and does not shift weight too far to either to the stern or bow. Your boat builder is the best person to discuss the rigging of the wing of a particular type of hull.

7.3.3 A Final Note

Rigging. Art? Science? Both. Learning about your boat is an important way to develop understanding of the technical side of sculling and can be fun. Rigging should be done with care and once you arrive at a good general rig that works for you spend time rowing it before you begin to make too many readjustments. When you need to make changes only do one thing at a time so you can observe the effect of the change. The final note, once you have measured; measure again.

Chapter 8: Race Preparation

Racing is hard work. It requires discipline, dedication, risk-taking, and mental toughness. There are many reasons why athletes race and engage in performance-oriented training. Knowing why you race is part of setting goals and better prepares you for achieving those goals. Here are a few reasons you may want to consider if you are making a decision whether or not to compete:

- Racing can be very satisfying. The more effort you have put into preparing for an event, the greater rewards you receive for rowing a well-executed race.
- Effort equals achievement. In rowing, if you work hard, train wisely, and stay healthy you will improve and get faster.
- Racing is fun. Being part of the racing scene is an ideal way to enjoy camaraderie with other rowers your age. Although competition is often fierce, most masters share great respect for one another.
- Testing the unknown. Unless you enter a race and go down the course you won't know your potential. When you sit at the starting line, you never know exactly what's going to happen between the start and the finish. You have to row the race to find out and gain the experience.

8.1 Setting Goals

As an athlete, you must have an overall plan and an idea how you are going to achieve what you want. Your goals and visions are what fuel you during those tough moments in training or a race when you have to push your limits. Your goals can be stated in simple language and be based on your past performances, rate of improvement, competition dates and priority of training factors such as physical, technical, tactical, or psychological elements. You may set subjective goals and objective goals.

Subjective goals are more open by nature such as:

1) Feel acceleration of body weight through the entire stroke.
2) Develop better sense of rhythm at higher stroke rates.
3) Increase ability to focus on one stroke at a time.

Objective goals are distinctly measurable such as:

1) Improve 2k erg score from 7:20 to 7:15 by March 01.
2) Decrease body fat percentage from 17 to 15% in 4 months.
3) Place top 3 in the Women's D-1x at FISA Master World Championships.

Write your goals down in your logbook. State 3 subjective goals and 3 objective goals for the upcoming season. Always begin your goal with a verb.

Draw up a plan. You need to make a road map, generally and specifically, how you will get from where you are today to where you want to be. Setting short-term weekly or monthly goals will help you break your goals down into achievable steps. Review your goals and determine what you need to do for each. Set yourself up for success at each stage to build confidence and reach your long-term goal. You can't row a 2k erg in 7:15 until you have accomplished 7:19, 7:18, or 7:16. Put one foot in front of the other at every stage.

Collaborate with a coach or advisor. A good coach can give you valuable objective advice combined with a more informed perspective. Helping you determine realistic goals and outlining a plan together are other benefits of coaching. Written materials and the Internet provide good training information but may or may not be specifically tailored to meet your needs.

Be flexible. After you outline a plan realize that it is simply that – an outline. At times outside stresses may interfere with your plan or your response to the volume of training may be different that you anticipate necessitating modifications. You may need to incorporate more rest or more work depending on whether you are making positive adaptations to your training.

Make wise daily decisions based on your goals. Many of you have limited time schedules and must prioritize your training elements. Spend time on the elements that improve your rowing.

8.2 Racing Choices

On water or land, race distances for masters may range from the 500-meter dash to 20-mile open water races to 100,000 meters on the erg. Each distance has its own physiological and psychological demands necessitating specific preparation for each type of event. The distances you choose to race is often influenced by your own physical attributes, strengths, and likes.

8.2.1 Water: 1000 meters

The majority of masters races held in the late spring and summer season take place over 1000 meters. This is the international and national-level racing distance. Although the race is comparatively short, lasting 3-5 minutes, it is an extremely demanding distance that can push heart rates to near maximum. This distance lends itself to high racing tempos of 32-42 strokes per minute and produces high levels of lactic acid in the muscles in late stages of the race. Requiring approximately 130-150 strokes, 1000-meter races begin from a standing start usually on a 6-lane buoyed course with racers rowing side-by-side. Speed and power work superimposed on a good aerobic base are important elements of training for this event in order to have good starting acceleration and a finishing sprint. Technical proficiency at high rates and mental preparedness also factor in as racing requirements because there is rarely time to recover from mishaps such as a poor start, missed strokes, or crabs.

8.2.2 Water: 2000 meters

The international, senior, and collegiate racing distance is 2000 meters. These races are held during the spring and summer. Club and international championships are typically held at the end of the summer. The race time can last from 5 1/2 to 8 1/2 minutes depending on the boat class you are in. This distance requires a highly developed aerobic system and strength-endurance. Heart rates can reach near maximum and races are rowed at tempos between 32-38 strokes per minute with higher rates during the start and sprint. 2000-meters races start from a standing start and are conducted on a six-lane buoyed course.

8.2.3 Water: 5000 meters

Head-style races present a different variety of racing from that of 1000 meters. These longer endurance events take place on rivers and lakes in the late summer and through the fall. The start is a moving start with each sculler rowing in single file, head-to-head, spaced approximately 15 seconds apart. Scullers chase down their opponents while racing the clock over the designated course. Steering, passing, and personal tactics all figure largely in head racing success. Events may last from 20-30 minutes and stroke rates in a single range from 26-33 strokes per minute. Aerobic and anaerobic threshold training is significant for this distance to maintain even pacing over the entire distance; heart rates will tend to be 85-95% of maximum.

8.2.4 Water: Marathons

Races covering 10 miles or more fall into the class of races closer to the half-marathon or marathon. Training for these races requires high volume, low intensity mileage with the bulk of training done at 70-75% effort. Charting your course and preparing the right food and fluids can be decisive in these types of events. Eating and drinking should be practiced in training to devise a system that requires the least disruption to your speed. Open water races challenge currents, water conditions and require a hearty mental character when the going gets tough.

8.2.5 Land: 2000 meters

The standard contested indoor rowing distance is 2000 meters. This too is an extremely challenging middle distance event that can last from 6-9 minutes. Training requires a strong aerobic base combined with a high anaerobic threshold as the main performance determinant. Improving the muscle's buffering system and ability to tolerate lactic acid are other aspects of training that improve performance over 2000 meters.

8.2.6 Land: Ultra-distance

Long distance indoor racing events are on the rise. Currently there are age group world records established for the marathon, 42,195 meters, and the 100,000-meter row. Much like training on the water, these distances require high volume, low intensity work to build the aerobic capabilities needed to row the several hours it may take to complete.

8.3 Planning for Race Day

In addition to your physical and mental training for race day, there are many logistics that need to be taken care of when you compete. Being organized before the day of the race will decrease stress and make sure you have everything you need to concentrate and row your best. Here are some important points:

1. Submit your entry form and entry fee on time.
2. Make hotel reservations in advance, if needed.
3. Plan adequate travel time so you have a chance to rest and relax before you race. If you need to fly and change time zones, allow one day at the site for every hour of change.
4. Collect any information you need about the race site ahead of time.
5. Make any boat repairs or rigging adjustments at home so you have a chance to row it before race day.
6. Have a supply of healthy snacks and water with you in the event that there is a poor choice of food at the regatta site.

Before traveling to a race it is easy to forget important items. Use the Race Day Travel List to make sure you have everything you need.

Race Day Travel List

Equipment

Car Rack	o
Boat Rack	o
Boat Cover	o
Boat	o
Seat	o
Foot stretchers	o
Riggers	o
Oars	o
Boat Slings	o
Tie Down Straps	o
Speedcoach	o
Bow Markers	o
Tool Box	o
Boat Towel	o
Water Bottle	o
Seat Pad	o
Fin	o
Spare Collars Oarlock	o
Duct Tape	o

Clothing

Racing Suit/Shorts	o
Tights	o
Wind shirt/pants	o
Rain Gear	o
Sweat shirt/pants	o
Dry Clothes	o
Change of Shoes	o
Jacket	o
Hat/bandana	o

Miscellaneous

Road Map	o
Hotel Information	o
Entry Confirmation	o
Race Site Directions	o
Food & Snacks	o
Water & Juices	o
Sunscreen	o
Sunglasses	o
Blanket/Lawn chair	o

Chapter 9: Race Strategy

How you prepare to execute a race needs to be planned and practiced well in advance of the actual race day. You must know what your focus will be for each segment of the race in order to maximize your potential in a given competitive situation. Initially, you must consider certain factors before you can draw up an effective race plan.

Tactics in rowing refer to the plan used for the actual competition. Tactics are a function of technique and tactical preparation is the way you ready yourself to meet certain objectives in the competition. In addition to your own skill level, it is helpful to know the racing tactics of your opponents – physically and psychologically, the environment of the competition, and the rules of the event. The following considerations will provide you with insight towards designing a race plan that will fit both your personality and physical attributes. Answer honestly; you are only as good as your weakest link.
Strengths and weaknesses?

9.1 Physiological

How high is your level of aerobic power?
Is your endurance level as good as your anaerobic (sprinting) ability?
Are you fit aerobically; able to maintain a high base speed but lack sprinting speed in the last 500 meters?
Are you quick in the first half but lose speed the second half?
Does your leg drive remain strong the entire race?
Are you fast or slow out of the starting blocks?
Can you row a high enough stroke rate in the body of the race?

Review each 500 meters of the race and identify your strong points and your weak points. Determining your patterns identify areas you need to work on.

9.2 Psychological

What is your level of motivation to succeed?
Are you willing to pay the price to reach your goals?
Are you good at sprinting to catch up in the last 500 meters?
Do you give up when someone passes you?

How aggressive are you?
Do you have the confidence you need to row from behind?
What motivates you?
Can you visualize the race before it happens?
Can you see yourself winning?
Do you believe in your training program?
What is the most difficult segment of the race?
What is your favorite part of the race?

9.3 Technical

Are you strong into a head wind but unable to hold it together to row well in a tail wind?
Do you like to row a higher stroke rate?
Do you have difficulty raising your rate to a racing beat?
Do you lose your technique when you get tired?
Are you able to keep your hands and upper body relaxed?
Do you have good blade work throughout the race?
Are you able to transition your stroke rates up and down smoothly as dictated by your race plan?
Do you catch crabs when you get tense?
Are you confident in your technical abilities?

9.4 Address Your Weaknesses

Determine the aspects of your race you need to improve. For example, if you have a poor start, give the first 250 m more attention in practice. If you have a weak last 500 m, devise a plan to bolster your motivation and speed for the final sprint of the race. Include reminders during the race such as "10 strokes for sharp catches" or "10 strokes for clean releases" to keep your technique intact.

9.5 Know Your Performance Capability

Your race plan must work within your present level of capability. Know your times for 500 m/1000 m time trials in practice to determine your base speed. Be realistic and plan a race dependent on your demonstrated abilities. You need to practice race pace tempo during your workouts.

9.6 Determine Your Base Speed

You must learn what your maximum "cruising speed" is for the body of a race over the set distance you will be racing. Your base speed for 1000 m is your average split per 500 m in good conditions. Time trials need to be rowed periodically to help you determine your optimum stroke rating and pace over the same distance. If you do not use a speed device in your boat use a determined distance near your boathouse, which you can easily repeat and time. Ideally, the most efficient way to cover the racecourse is by rowing even splits (the same time per 500 meters) versus varying boat speed up and down during the race.

Race planning for single scullers relies heavily on your individual preferences. Do you need a structured plan, stroke by stroke, or simply a few points of technical focus at transition points in the race? In doubles and quads, you must experiment with different race plans as a team and to see what maximizes your potential and motivation. All scullers need to know what to expect during the race and be prepared for key moves.

- Approach the race plan in 250 m or 500 m segments.
- Count how many strokes it takes you to cover a 500 m distance.
- Decide where you need to make your major moves.
- Determine your technical focal points: For example: clean releases, keeping your head up, quick catches etc.
- Know what key words or commands will identify important transitions. A simple "Up" may be a command to start your final sprint in a coxless boat or "Now" may signify settling to your base rate. You must determine what works best for you.

9.7 Sample 1000-meter Race Plan

0-500 meters:
Start: 5 strokes (3/4, 1/2, 3/4, full, full) be very short and quick on the first 3
15 strokes high
20 strokes for rhythm/base speed
10 strokes for quick hands
5 strokes to check your course
Power 10 (will move you through the 500)

501-1000 meters:
20 strokes for good catches

5 to focus in the boat, prepare for sprint
20 strokes, take the stroke rate up one
10 strokes, take the stroke rate up one
10 strokes, final sprint to line

9.8 Sample 2000-meter Race Plan

0-500 meters:

Start: 5 strokes (3/4, 1/2, 3/4, full, full)
25 strokes high, quick legs, limited body swing
20 strokes to lengthen and set rhythm
10 strokes to sit up tall
10 strokes for clean releases

501-1000 meters:

Power 10, rating up one to move through the 500
20 strokes for rhythm
Power 10 to stay aggressive
20 strokes for focus on catches

1001-1500 meters:

5 strokes to check your course and prepare for a major move
20 strokes to move/respond/hold other crews off
20 strokes for rhythm
10 strokes to sit up tall
10 strokes for clean releases

1501-2000 meters:

Focus 10 moving into the last 500
Acceleration 10 (3/4, 3/4, 3/4, +7)
5 strokes to prepare for final sprint
20 strokes, take the stroke rate up one
20 final strokes, take the stroke rate up one every five to the finish line

9.9 Standing Starts

A standing start is considered to be the first 5 strokes of a race taken from a stationary position at the beginning of a 1000 m or 2000 m event. The main goal of the start is to pry the boat away from the starting line without "kicking" the boat sternward and accelerate the boat up to full speed as the initial short strokes are lengthened.

A clean start can boost your confidence in the early phases of a race and being first off the line is for some an important tactic to place them in position to watch the other challenging boats. There is a saying though, "You don't win the race at the start but you can certainly lose it" meaning crabs, missed strokes, and bad timing can put you way behind before you even get off the line.

Initially, perform starts at low stroke rates and power application to maintain relaxation but build up to race pace starts as soon as you can. Start from the catch position, blades squared and anchored just below the surface of the water. Care and time should be taken to pattern the proper motions before progressing towards more intensity. Most importantly, concentrate on only one point at a time when working on starts and include a few at the end of every practice.

9.9.1 Practice These Start Sequences:

- 5 x 1 stroke: 3/4 slide.
- 5 x 2 strokes: 3/4 slide,1/2 slide.
- 5 x 3 strokes: 3/4 slide, 1/2 slide, 3/4 slide.
- 5 x 4 strokes: 3/4, 1/2, 3/4, full slide.
- 5 x 5 strokes: 3/4, 1/2, 3/4, full, full slide.
- 5 x 10 strokes:3/4, 1/2, 3/4, full, full, paddle 5 strokes.

A start in the single requires a delicate balance of lightness and aggression to get away from the line quickly and maintain a straight course. Practice limited upper body swing and a loose hold on the handles to feel sharp and avoid tension. You may want to try a variation of 3/4, 3/4, 3/4, full, full for the first 5 strokes. Experiment to find that start that is most effective for you and feels most stable. Aim for rates between 35-45 spm.

9.10 Moving Starts

Moving starts are how you begin a headrace. Moving starts also provide a way to practice several starts consecutively without becoming fatigued. In cooler weather, multiple flying starts can keep you warm, avoiding chilling down between starts from a stand still and risking injury.
- Row on the paddle, flying starts are executed with the boat in motion.
- Take 3 strokes to build into a 5- stroke start. You may use a standard 3/4, 1/2, 3/4, full, full or a sequence you prefer.
- After the fifth stroke continue to row for 20 strokes then repeat 3 strokes to build + your 5-stroke start.
- Repeat 5 times. Emphasize unity in timing, sharpness, and swing in the boat.

This drill will help the single sculler build confidence doing racing starts at higher ratings. Practice a few starts daily at the end of your row.

9.11 Stroke Transitions

Transitions are changes from one stroke rate to another. These drills focus on raising the rating. A transition stroke should be precise and happen in one designated stroke. You must commit to it. To learn good transitions use the speed of your hands away from your body as you complete the release and the emphasis of a strong leg drive to define your rating shift. The following 40-stroke pieces are some of the stroke varieties you can practice:

- Row at base stroke rate, full pressure for 20. Increase the rating 2 SPM for the last 20. (Target rates: 26-28, 28-30, 30-32, 32-34).

- Row at base stroke rate, full pressure, for 20. Increase the rating 2 SPM for 10, then again 2 SPM for 10. (Target rates: 26-28-30, 28-30-32, 30-32-34, 32-34-36).
- Row at base stroke rate, full pressure for 10. Increase the rating 2 SPM each 10 for a total of 40 strokes. (Target rates: 26-28-30-32, 28-30-32-34, 30-32-34-36, 32-34-36-38).

- Row at base stroke rate, full pressure for 20. Increase the rating 2 SPM every 5 strokes for a total of 40. (Target rates: 28-30-32-34-36, 30-32-34-36-38, 32-34-36-38-40).

In a single, practicing your rating shifts can help you find that extra gear when you need it in a race. Learning what works best for you and making rating changes purposeful will give you more confidence to follow and execute your race plan

9.12 Steering: Buoyed Lanes

Going straight is the main goal when rowing on a buoyed course. Any deviation in your course is disconcerting if you hit buoys with your blade disrupting your rhythm and adding extra meters onto your race distance. Few people have the opportunity to row daily on a set course so practicing your steering at home is necessary to prepare to go straight.

When you row steady get into the habit of steering off a point on the shore. Get used to keeping your stern on a fixed point as you row away from it. When you do a start, pay close attention to whether you go straight or deviate to one side. Correct any asymmetries in your start so you get away from the line without having to make adjustments in your first 20 strokes.

Make slight corrections as soon as you sense you are going off course to stay in the center of the lane. Do not wait until you are already hitting the lane markers before you react. Keep your head up and use your peripheral vision to stay centered in the lane. Arriving at the course the day before will give you a chance to row over the course a few times and get the sense of rowing in a lane. During your race warm-up, you can usually row into your designated lane as soon as the race before your event is started. Practice some starts in the direction of the race.

9.13 Steering: Head Racing

In terms of steering, head races present very different challenges than 1000- or 2000-meter racing. Sprint racing is conducted in buoyed lanes necessitating a straight course but head races vary from race to race and often include considerations such as: current strength, turns, and wind direction. In a head race situation a good course will get you to the finish line without rowing extra distance or being slowed by current. Here are some tips to keep in mind:
Ideally, arrive at the racecourse in time to row over the course. Otherwise study the course map carefully to be aware of curves or snags.

Study where the markers are placed and determine the shortest course for the overall race. Markers may not always represent the best course and may be placed simply to designate course boundaries. Inquire about places where the current of the river can vary. Aim to have current help you pick up speed rather than rowing against it. Look for important landmarks to line up your stern for various sections of a racecourse in order to point the bow in the correct direction. Make steering corrections when the blades are in the water.

Scullers can change their course by altering the extension of the handles at the catch. Slightly lengthening the arc of one oar handle will allow the boat to turn to the opposite direction at the initiation of the drive. This will keep disturbance of the drive phase to a minimum. If you are using a rudder make corrections during the drive. Check your course by glancing over your shoulder during the drive if you are in a sculling boat. Some scullers also prefer using a mirror mounted on a hat or headband.

Practice the alternation of looking over right and left shoulders for 10-20 strokes during steady rows to get comfortable with this. In a race situation, look out of the boat only as much as you need to for safety, steering, and passing other boats. Excessive steering will decrease your boat speed.

9.13 Race Performance Evaluation

You learn something from every racing experience. It is as important for you to know what didn't work, as well as, what did work. Spending a few minutes to write down the details of a race can serve as a very valuable resource when you are preparing for a peak event. As soon as you can after your race record in your log book:

Date:
Event:
Result:
How did you feel about your performance?
What was your goal for this event?
Did you achieve your goal?
What was your focus coming into the event?
Did you execute your focal points?
Did you feel confident going into the race?
What was your warm-up routine?
When did you feel your best during the race?
When did you feel your worst?
Did anything unexpected happen during the race?
What would you improve on for the next race?
Plan:
Sample Race Evaluation
Date: 01 August 1999
Event: B-1x heat: Canadian Henley
Result: 4th

There were segments of the race that I felt were much improved from Nationals but I felt that my last 250 m was not as dynamic or full of fire as I need it to be. I seem to be able to maintain speed at that point but do not seem to really increase speed to fight for positions. Warm-up on the water went well. It was very hot, head wind conditions, the water was not too rough but some rippling on the surface. I paddled 750 m up to the start, turned in the direction of the course- focus was relaxed hands even though I was bouncing around from boat washes. Did 2 x (3to build+ 5/5/5 high) plus 1 x (start+ 5). Then paddled 5-6 minutes and did one more start closer to the start of the previous race. Sat in the boat about 5 minutes before going into the start.

0-500 m – Lined up easily at start, stayed straight, Attention/green light/buzzer was fast. First 3 strokes felt slow but I was 2nd or 3rd out, had to steer a little in the first 10 strokes to stay off port buoys. Fell short of 25 high it was more like 20 high then lengthen/rhythm. Was in the front group after 40 strokes. Readjusted my fingers on starboard oar a few times to keep my wrists up at the release, tried to not pull through too far on starboard. Technique calls focused on 1/2 blades to stay light.

500-1000 m – I started my 10/5/10 about 1100 m because I had to make sure my course was OK, I never hit any buoys but did swerve a little. I really emphasized quick but unhurried releases, light blade work, tapping the boat along, final sprint needs to be more defined, it feels hard for me to get the rating up dramatically, I feel like I just stay the same speed. I want to be more aggressive at the end. I was 4th. My time 4:03.

My goal was to get to the semifinal, did not qualify. I wanted to stay firm in the release and in the water, keep blade work clean and shallow, stay in control, not panic and choke the handle, I wanted clear concentration and to stay in the present, to avoid self-talk positive or negative, to not be judgmental of my performance during the race, I wanted a clean start and to steer relatively well.

I felt fairly determined, pretty charged up, calm before the start, in control, focused on the task at hand, and fairly confident but not totally.

Most of race plan/steering was followed. Did not follow completing the full 5 stroke start/25 high- did total of 20 not 30, last 500 m was unsure of counting strokes after the 10/5/10 until the finish line. I went off course slightly twice and caught a blade once – I just thought clean blades, quick hands.

For the next race: Better start, attacking more in race mentality, decrease self-talk, improve race plan for the last 500 m by perfecting the final sprint.

Chapter 10: Tapering

During the final preparation for a major competition, you need to feel rested, quick, and strong. To accomplish this, a taper is often used. A taper is a period of drastically reduced training volume that lasts from 7 to 21 days prior to the year's major competition. Unfortunately, there are no published studies on tapering and rowing performance. This is partially because changing wind and water conditions make it difficult to do accurate pre- and post-taper measures on competitive rowers. Therefore, much of the information used by rowing coaches and scientists comes from swimming, cycling and running.

The objective of training is to induce physiological and mechanical changes in an athlete so that their performance improves. During periods of high-volume training common to rowers training adaptations are often masked by the fatigue of incomplete recovery between sessions (Figure 6). While club rowers typically don't use the same volume as international rowers they have other stressors such as family and work that can contribute to incomplete recovery. The main purpose of a taper is to allow the physiological systems to completely recover and adapt. In order to plan a taper training volume, intensity, frequency, and duration all need to be considered.

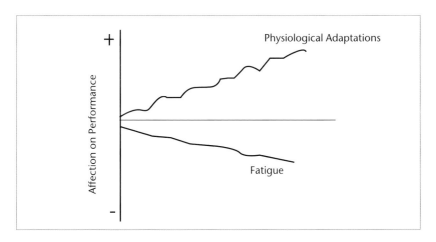

Figure 6: Fatigue can mask performance improvements

10.1 Volume

Volume is the total number of training hours per week. Some people like to use distance measures to keep track of volume but time is a more accurate indicator of the physiological stress training imposes. A reduction in volume is the main feature of a taper. Typically volume is reduced by 70-90%. If the work volume is relatively low, 4-8 hours of training per week, volume should be reduced by 70%. If training volume is above 8 hours per week a reduction of 80-90% is more appropriate.

A taper can either be progressive, meaning there is a gradual decrease in volume over the period of the taper, or it can be stepped, meaning there is a single decrease in volume for the duration of the taper. Progressive tapers seem to have a greater impact on performance than step tapers. This is probably due to detraining effects that occur when the rapid volume decrease used in step tapering is maintained for an extended period of time. While a progressive taper is the obvious choice for the major competition of the year, a step taper may be better for qualifying competitions and other less important events where the taper duration is much shorter.

10.2 Frequency

Training frequency refers to the number of training sessions per week. The reduction of training volume in a taper should not occur as the result of drastic changes in training frequency. Studies in which tapering has resulted in improved performance have typically decreased frequency by 20 to 50%. Several researchers have recommended that training frequency not be reduced by more than 20%. In other words if you were doing 5 hour-long training sessions per week during the taper you would want to gradually work down to 4 20-minutes sessions.

While this may seem like a waste of time to show up at the boat house, get changed, rig your boat and haul it down to the water for a 20-minute training session it is the most effective way of performing a taper. The reasons why a reduction in frequency causes a decrease in performance is unclear, but may be related to decreased technical efficiency. As frequency of technical work is decreased there is probably some loss in technique that ultimately affects performance.

10.3 Intensity

Intensity during a taper is usually maintained or increased. There is a tendency for a greater proportion of the training to become race-specific type intervals. In rowing, this translates into increased training in categories III and II. The time period between the intervals should be long enough to maximize intensity. In a study that compared high intensity and low intensity tapers it was found that the physiological responses to the two tapers were similar but only the high intensity taper group showed an increase in performance. Training schedules that use intensities of less than 70% VO_2 max maintain or decrease performance during a taper, while schedules which use intensities of greater than 90% VO_2 max improve performance. The higher intensity training allows you to get used to higher stroke rates, allows you to work on race strategy and tactics, and psychologically gives you feelings of speed and power.

10.4 Duration

Since the training stimulus is greatly reduced during a taper, the duration of the taper can have an impact on the magnitude of performance improvements. Within 1 to 4 weeks of stopping training highly trained athletes start to show decreases in fitness. A group of Japanese researchers studied the effects of 21-, 28- and 42-day tapers on performance in highly trained swimmers. They found significant improvements in the 21- and 28-day groups but not the 42-day taper group.

The number of days needed to taper may be affected by training volume and intensity going into the taper and fitness level of the athlete. High performance international competitors need 21-28 days to completely recover from the huge volumes they use during training. There is anecdotal evidence that fitness can continue to improve for as much as 12 weeks following the Olympic games. If you are training less than 8 hours per week your taper should be 7-14 days long. Training more than 8 hours per week will require a taper of 10-21 days.

10.5 Special Considerations During a Taper

The taper period can be a time of high psychological stress for both the coach and athlete. Coaches tend to worry about the training that was done during the season, the duration of the taper, and many other things that arise prior to a major competition. It is important at this time of the year that the coach projects confidence both in what has been done during the season and in the taper. If the coach is openly worried about the athlete's preparation or starts making changes to a planned taper the athletes may begin to question their preparedness and ability to win.

Athletes handle the decreased training volume differently. Many athletes will enjoy the feelings of speed, power and renewed energy. Others have a tough time dealing with the decrease in volume. They worry about detraining and don't know how to cope with the extra time as a result of the decreased volume. A coach needs to be aware of the responses of each athlete, and be prepared to deal with the worriers.

Lightweight rowers need to pay attention to their weight during a taper. One of the adaptations to a taper is an increase in muscle glycogen storage. For every gram of glycogen stored in the muscle three grams of water are stored. This can result in a large increase in weight in a relatively short period of time. A certain amount of weight gain may be necessary if the athlete is to see performance improvements as a result of the taper.

The increased glycogen storage not only feeds the muscles during training but it is used as an energy source for other adaptations to occur.

Lightweight rowers have to carefully balance the amount of glycogen supercompensation that will improve performance with the amount of weight they can gain.

Strength training should be stopped when the taper begins. Strength can easily be maintained for the duration of the taper by doing high intensity intervals. If a taper is done for a minor competition strength training should be started again a couple of days after the race.

10.6 Sample 14 Day Taper

Day	Training
1	40 min CAT VI
2	5 x 500 m at race pace, 10 min paddle between
3	5 x 100 m starts, 20 minute paddle
4	3 x 750 m race pace with 10 minute paddle between pieces
5	40 min CAT VI
6	3 x 7 minutes at Anaerobic Threshold, 7 min rest between.
7	OFF
8	OFF
9	3 x 500 m at race pace
10	2 x 750 m at race pace, 20 minute paddle
11	30 min CAT VI
12	OFF
13	4 x 50 m starts, 15 min light paddle
14	Race Day

Chapter 11: Rest and Recovery

Rest is a training intensity that is overlooked in its importance. Rest is as critical to the success of your rowing as hard workouts. Working athletes face particular challenges fitting enough rest into their training programs. With active professional careers, frequent business travel, or family obligations, just getting workouts done can be a juggling act. With some thought and creativity, reaching a balanced training volume that produces good results is always possible. This chapter will discuss why you need to rest and sensible ways to incorporate rest into your training.

11.1 What is Fatigue?

Fatigue resulting from physical work reduces the capacity of the neuromuscular and metabolic systems to function. Neuromuscular fatigue involves the central nervous system, which alternates activity between nerve cell excitation and inhibition. Good performances happen from a controlled excited state of the nerve impulses. When fatigue develops nerve cells go into a state of inhibition and muscles work slower and weaker than normal. When an athlete starts to perform below average the nerve cells may be in a state of "inhibition of protection" and exhaustion. Prolonged training in this condition usually results in overtraining.

Metabolic sources of fatigue include the elevation of lactic acid in the blood, high blood acidosis, glycogen depletion, or carbohydrate store reduction. If muscle glycogen is not adequately supplied or the muscles are not fueled properly performance will decrease.

11.2 Overtraining Syndrome

When the work to recovery ratio is incorrect, you can enter an abnormal state of training referred to as overtraining. This results from continuing high intensity training when in an extended state of fatigue. The amount of recovery you need to build into your program depends upon your intensity of training; the higher the intensity, the longer recovery time required. If you do not recovery enough you remain in a fatigued state from workout to workout and exhaustion can result.

Physiological

- Abnormal ECG readings
- Heart discomfort on exertion
- Changes in blood pressure
- Changes in resting heart rate
- Changes in exercising heart rate
- Increased respiratory frequency
- Decreased body fat
- Increased O_2 at submax loads
- Elevated BMR
- Loss of appetite
- Muscle soreness/tenderness
- Increased aches and pains
- Tendon pains
- Muscle damage
- Headaches
- Chronic fatigue
- Shift in lactate curve towards the x axis

Immune Function

- Increased susceptibility to illness
- Swelling of lymph glands
- One day colds
- Minor scratches heal slowly
- Increased blood eosinophil count
- Flu-like illnesses
- Decreased total lymphocyte count

Performance

- Decreased performance
- Decreased strength
- Loss of coordination
- Technical errors increase
- Prolonged recovery
- Reduced tolerance of training load

Psychological

- Depression
- Apathy
- Emotional instability
- Fear of competition
- Personality changes
- Difficulty in concentrating
- Increased distractability

Biochemical

- Negative nitrogen balance
- Decreased bone mineral content
- Low free testosterone
- Delayed menarche
- Decreased hemoglobin
- Depressed muscle glycogen
- Elevated cortisol
- Increased urea concentration

Overtraining could perhaps be better translated as overstress. Training is only one of your activities of daily living; other stressors such as family, work, or finances combined with intense training loads can potentially push you beyond your healthy capacity to cope. Unless the existing stressors are addressed, a state of overtraining can continue for long periods of time, especially as you get older. The best approach is to take a preventive stance. Know and be candid with yourself when you begin to experience signs of overstress. Modify your activities to incorporate more rest and allow yourself to regain physical and psychological balance before you resume your normal schedule again.

Every athlete reacts differently to heavy fatigue; some get depressed easily, others catch frequent colds. If you are attentive to your body's signals and your feelings, you will learn to recognize the early warning signals that tell you to adjust your training accordingly. There are a battery of signs and symptoms of overtraining. Psychological symptoms are marked by a lack of confidence, decreased concentration, sensitivity to criticism, lack of initiative, decreased will power, a tendency towards isolation, and fear of competitions. Physical symptoms can become apparent as decreased coordination, the reappearance of a corrected mistake, muscle tension, decreased performance factors (speed, strength, endurance), slowed reaction time, and a slowed rate of recovery from session to session. Functional manifestations are insomnia, decreased appetite, elevated morning heart rate, heart rate recovery is longer than normal, muscle soreness, and a high propensity to infections.

Sympathetic overtraining refers to the overstressing of the emotional state of the athlete. Parasympathetic overtraining results from an increase in the central nervous system's inhibition processes and is from too high a volume of training. When training loads are abruptly increased, the body's ability to adapt at the cellular level is not adequate and either type of overtraining can occur. In either event, immediate attention needs to be paid to what you are experiencing and corrective actions must be taken. Training has to be reduced or possibly stopped. All participation in competitions should be temporarily cancelled and social obligations reduced to a minimum to allow rest.

Day	Muscle Soreness	Joint Soreness	Fatigue after Training	Desire to Train	General Fatigue	Quality of Sleep
Monday						
Tuesday						
Wednesday						
Thursday						
Friday						
Saturday						
Sunday						
Average						

Figure 7: Overtraining Sheet

Rate each of the items on a scale from 1-10 (low to high) according to how you feel. If the average value for two or more items drops by more than 1.5 points, overtraining may be starting to occur and the training program should be adjusted.

179

11.3 Recovering from Training or Racing

When the balance between work and rest is correct, you make obvious positive progress in your sculling and you feel good about it. Maintaining balance between private life, professional life, and athletic endeavors needs constant attention; it is a dynamic process. As you age, your ability to recover takes more time and this needs to be taken into serious consideration when balancing hard sessions, easy sessions, and adequate recovery time.

After your daily workout, you experience some level of fatigue. The more you are fatigued, the stronger the symptoms may be after the session: poor coordination or slowed or weakened muscle contractions. Physiological fatigue is usually combined with psychological or emotional fatigue, especially after racing. Using a variety of recovery techniques built into your training plan will help you train better and prevent injuries. You regularly need to "sharpen the saw" so your blade cuts through the water with quality.

Active Rest

Recovery through movement or active rest facilitates faster recovery than total rest due to increased circulation. When an alternate exercise is used, it allows the fatigued muscle groups to rest and the resulting recovery rate is faster. For a sculler, good choices would be 30 minutes of swimming, 1 hour of cycling or tennis, or a 30-minute easy walk or jog.

Passive Rest

This type of recovery includes activities such as reading, watching television, going to the movies, going to a concert, going out to dinner, or lying in the sun. You are relatively stationary and just taking it easy.

Sleep

Relaxed sleep is the body's main form of restoration. A sculler that keeps an active training schedule realistically requires 9 hours of sleep per night to adequately recover from day to day. It is highly recommended to go to sleep on a regular schedule in a dark, quiet room with lots of fresh air circulating. Short naps are also very restorative between training sessions but most of your sleeping should be done at night to insure adequate deep sleep.

Massage

Massage effectively assists the elimination of toxic substances from the tissues, stimulates circulation, and decreases muscle tension. There are over 300 massage modalities and techniques. The primary focus here is on sports massage, which is the precise application of manual maneuvers employed at different times in the training schedule. For example, a pre-event massage will decrease muscle tension yet keep the body and mind ready for competition.

A post-event flush is a total body massage taking up to 30-40' given soon after a hard training session or race. A flush is defined by the type of superficial strokes used: jostling, compression, effleurage, and spreading which help to increase the elimination of lactic acid and other metabolic waste products. Sessions conducted on rest days are called maintenance massages and are reserved for deep tissue work and targeted at injury prevention.

Hydrotherapy

Water therapies help the mind and body to recover and be restored. Hot showers and baths relax muscles, increase circulation, and improve the quality of sleep. Contrast showers that alternate hot and cold water stimulate circulation and saunas allow for vasodilation and perspiration, which helps to eliminate toxins from the muscle cell. Toxins cause fatigue to linger and negatively affect CNS stimulation. Saunas taken weekly for a minimum of 15 minutes produce effects which would normally require 2 hours of rest to achieve. Cross-country skiers routinely build time for saunas into their training plans. A full session can consist of 3 x 10-15 minute sessions. After each bout you must immediately rinse in a cold water shower blending it to warm to create the desired contrast effect. Once wrapped in a robe, relax and cool down for 10-15 minutes before the next round. Drinking lots of fresh water between sessions helps the cleansing process.

Psychological Restoration

The goal is to reduce stress and feel good about yourself. Choose activities that you truly find relaxing, whether it be watching a film or hiking in the mountains for a change of scenery. Be sure to regularly incorporate simple things you like to do into your day. Let your mind wander away from training or work concerns and feel refreshed.

Athletic Lifestyle

Living an athletic lifestyle requires commitment. It means getting enough sleep, eating an appropriate diet, keeping an organized schedule, avoiding excessive alcohol or caffeine, and maintaining balance between your activities of daily life. Though these are ideals, making wise choices in everyday matters accumulate and can make a great contribution to your overall health and your ability to row.

11.4 Incorporating Rest Into Your Training

Balancing training and rest is an art. Here are a few things to keep in mind:

- Increase your training gradually and progressively. Avoid extreme, rapid changes in your program. If you increase your volume you must decrease the intensity and vice versa. If you train more you need to rest more.
- Give your body time to adapt cellularly to the training stresses that you place on it. If you are not sure you are completely recovery, rest an extra day or modify your training session to be lighter. Be conservative.
- Employ a periodized training plan that varies the workload on a weekly, monthly, and yearly basis.
- Hire a coach to design your training plan with you.
- Keep variety in your program. Row with other people, in different boats, travel, and do cross-training.

Take one full day off from training each week. The ideal is a day you do not work either to have a true rest day. When in doubt: rest. Aim for peaks in your performance instead of breakdown.

Keep a logbook to monitor your training and response to stress. In your entries record the date, day of the week, resting heart rate, body weight, workout, total distance or time, injuries, subjective feelings, and any other important notes.

Photo & Illustration Credits

Cover Photo: Sportpressefoto Bongarts, Hamburg
Cover Design: Birgit Engelen
Photos: Chris Scott, Edward McNeely, Marlene Royle
Illustrations: Mike Reed, Sylvain Lemaire

Fit & Healthy

Georg Neumann/
Arndt Pfützner/Anneliese Berbalk
Successful Endurance Training

Athletes, trainers, coaches and medical supervisors will find ideas for their own fields in the detailed presentation of the training environment from the point of view of both sports medicine and sports methodology. Effort and benefit in training should be balanced according to the individual ability of athletes and the amount of time available. The requirements for increasing training effectiveness are discussed in detail.

320 pages
16 photos, 50 tables
About 90 illustrations
Paperback, 14.8 x 21 cm
ISBN 1-84126-004-5
£ 12.95 UK/$ 17.95 US/
$ 25.95 CDN/€ 18.90

Georg Neumann
Nutrition in Sport

The book makes recommendations for physiologically useful dietary planning before, during and after training in various sports. It also examines risk-prone groups in sports nutrition. The emphasis is on presenting the latest research on the effects of carbohydrates and proteins and other active substances, such as vitamins and minerals, on performance training. Particular attention is paid to the intake of food and fluids under special conditions such as training in heat, in the cold and at high altitudes.

208 pages, Two-colour print
Some full-colour photos
Paperback, 14.8 x 21 cm
ISBN 1-84126-003-7
£ 12.95 UK/$ 17.95 US/
$ 25.95 CDN/€ 18.90

XD2K/Anz1 02/02

MEYER
& MEYER
SPORT

MEYER & MEYER Verlag | Von-Coels-Straße 390 | D-52080 Aachen, Germany | Fax +49 (0)241-9 58 10-10

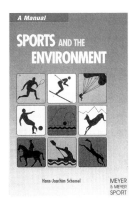